CW01213040

AFTER YOU'RE GONE

AFTER YOU'RE GONE

CHELSEA GIOVINCO

Copyright © 2024 by Chelsea Giovinco.

All rights reserved. No part of this publication may be reproduced, distributed, or transmitted in any form or by any electronic or mechanical means, including information storage and retrieval systems, without a prior written permission from the publisher, except by reviewers, who may quote brief passages in a review, and certain other noncommercial uses permitted by the copyright law.

Library of Congress Control Number: 2024921785

ISBN: 979-8-89228-181-2   (Paperback)
ISBN: 979-8-89228-182-9   (Hardcover)
ISBN: 979-8-89228-183-6   (eBook)

Book Ordering Information:
Atticus Publishing
548 Market St PMB 70756
San Francisco, CA 94104
(888) 208-9296
info@atticuspublishing.com
www.atticuspublishing.com

Printed in the United States of America

Contents

PROLOGUE – JUNE 2024 1

CHAPTER 1 – JUNE 2024 3

CHAPTER 2 – APRIL 2002 15

CHAPTER 3 – JUNE 2024 25

CHAPTER 4 – JUNE 2024 45

CHAPTER 5 – APRIL 2003 63

CHAPTER 6 – JUNE 2024 68

CHAPTER 7 – JUNE 2024 78

CHAPTER 8 – MARCH 2004 87

CHAPTER 9 – JULY 2004 91

CHAPTER 10 – JUNE 2024 96

CHAPTER 11 – JUNE 2024 117

CHAPTER 12 – JUNE 2024 126

CHAPTER 13 – FEBRUARY 2024 135

CHAPTER 14 – JUNE 2024 140

CHAPTER 15 – JUNE 2024 154

EPILOGUE – ONE WEEK LATER 173

To My Husband, Mike

My sounding board, my support system, my best friend –
I wouldn't have gotten this far without you

In Memory of My Dad, Ralph Pagano

Without you, I may never have had the courage to break out of my shell and explore the depths of my passion for telling stories through music and words

PROLOGUE – JUNE 2024

RACHEL

I gaze wearily at the people surrounding me, feeling utterly drained. The grief is overwhelming. I feel each person's sadness and denial just as strongly as I feel my own. The sea of black and my intense emotions greatly contrast with today's clear blue sky and bright warm sun. I guess that's how it works, though. My mom used to tell me in times like this that the contrast provides the perspective needed when all you can see is darkness. I'm under the impression that it's just the universe's idea of a cruel joke.

Everyone here loved her. As I scan the crowd, I try to name each person and recall their connection to Evelyn.

Across from where she lived, there is a pharmacy where she went to pick up all of her medicine. I spot Jennifer, the owner, standing off to the side of the large crowd. Over the past 5 months of her illness, my mom brought Jennifer homemade treats every time she had to stop by.

I see our neighbor, Glenn, sitting alone in a chair close to the casket. Even though he hardly ever steps out into the "real world," he and my mom were each other's only true daily company. This became especially true after his wife passed away a few years ago, and Abby and I moved out.

Other neighbors, coworkers, people she knew from the supermarket, or coffee shop, crowd the small area of the cemetery surrounding her gravesite. I can only scan the crowd for so long before it hits me that my sister, Abby, really didn't show.

Before I can dwell on that fact, my train of thought is interrupted by shadows moving behind the trees in the distance. It could be an animal or perhaps some kids from the nearby neighborhood, but I let my attention linger for a few extra moments while I pretend it's really Abby watching from afar. I try to imagine all the reasons she might have for keeping her distance, but I come up empty.

I am snapped back to reality when Jennifer approaches me, awkwardly wrapping me in a sympathetic hug while saying her goodbyes. Everyone else follows shortly after.

Once everyone has finally left, I stand and approach my mother. As I kiss her coffin, say my final goodbyes, and drop pieces of our shared memories into the dirt below, I can only hope that my sister gets her chance to say her final goodbyes and make peace with our mom in her own way.

CHAPTER 1 – JUNE 2024

RACHEL

As I walk into my apartment, I immediately trip over a pile of mail that's been thrown through the slot on my door. I haven't been in my apartment for weeks, except to grab extra clothes or check that the building hasn't burned down.

I have never felt like more of a walking disaster than I do right now, like I'm the epitome of a human cyclone. Dishes are still piled in the sink from the rushed meals I've had over the past few weeks. The smell coming from the trash can tells me I should've taken it out before I left. A three-week-old pizza box sits open on the counter, dirty clothes are strewn across the couch and floor, and a thick layer of dust covers every surface. Every square inch of my small studio apartment is an overwhelming mess.

Living alone is usually something I relish. There is no one to answer to or tiptoe around, and no one else's mess to contend with, which inevitably drives me insane. At least the mess here is my own to deal with.

I don't even have a bedroom door; instead, a makeshift divider, inspired by a scene from my favorite Disney movie, separates my bed from my couch. I have positioned my TV so that I can watch it comfortably from either spot, and I am always anywhere from three to five steps away from my tiny kitchen. Essentially, I eat, sleep, and relax all in the same area.

The lack of extra room makes my place feel cozier and more secure somehow, and I've managed just fine on my own for years. Though, it would've been nice to have someone who could have picked up the slack for me these past few weeks, or at least helped with the dusting.

I had lived with my mom, Evelyn, and my sister, Abigail, my entire life, up until a few years ago when Abby and I both decided we needed our own space. I moved into my first apartment around the same time Abby went off to college. While I had lived with my mom and commuted to the nearby State College of Florida, Abby preferred to experience the on-campus lifestyle. It marked the first time the three of us weren't always together. After Abby graduated early last Fall, she got her own apartment. Despite our moves taking us 10 minutes apart from each other, we still managed to see each other almost as often as before.

Before she was diagnosed with Stage 4 pancreatic cancer, my mom lived alone, too. Since then, there appears to be a near-constant stream of neighbors, friends, co-workers, and even strangers stopping by with meals or staying with her on her bad days. My mom had that infectious personality where anyone who met her instantly became her best friend. We were different in that way. She was the mom who befriended all the other school moms when Abby and I were younger, even the obnoxious ones everyone else tried their hardest to avoid. She participated in all the school fundraisers and volunteered to chaperone all our field trips. She needed to be social, and she thrived around others.

Despite receiving a terminal diagnosis, my mom insisted on attending every single treatment. She refused to go down without a fight, even if the outcome seemed inevitable. She showed up to every treatment, every battle, mentally and physically tough despite knowing the war was already lost. I argued with her about it constantly, because, while losing her was the worst thing imaginable, I didn't want to see her sacrifice all quality of life in her final months.

One day after a particularly rough treatment session, my mom began sobbing into my shoulder as I questioned whether all of it was worth enduring for only a few extra weeks. She explained in a tone that left no room for argument that all she wanted was more time, as much as she could get, no matter how uncomfortable she felt. She didn't care about how she was feeling; all she wanted was every possible minute on this earth with her girls.

After that day, I chose to keep my thoughts to myself. I wasn't going to remind her that only one of her girls was currently present. Abby would come back. She had to.

Over the next couple of weeks, her condition deteriorated rapidly. I stayed by her side to ensure she made it to her appointments, ultimately becoming her full-time caregiver. Despite the grim circumstances, I found myself given the opportunity to cherish every final moment in ways most people don't get to experience.

During her final weeks, we shared laughter reminiscing about the times I embarrassed myself in front of my crushes, cherished our favorite childhood memories, and discussed our top 10 lists of favorite music, movies, concerts, and plays we went to. We also had difficult conversations about the life she was leaving behind and the experiences she wouldn't be there to witness. Despite the pain, she wanted to hear about my plans for the future. These moments, though bittersweet, are ones I will always treasure.

My mom passed away five days ago.

Stepping over the mess on my apartment floor, I divert my attention from the kitchen, promising myself I'll clean it all up later as I make my way to the couch. I turn on my TV, hoping to find some type of distraction to pull me out of my head, but nothing seems to do the trick. After aimlessly scrolling through every streaming service I subscribe to for about twenty minutes, I settle on rewatching Dirty Dancing for the hundredth time. About ten minutes into reciting every line of the movie word-for-word, I realize this isn't quite the distraction I need. Suddenly, the apartment suddenly feels way too small and too messy to find any solace in.

An image of the beautiful trail right behind my apartment complex pops into my head, and now a run sounds like just the kind of distraction I need. Maybe it will allow me to come back with a clearer head. I need my apartment to not be so overwhelming, but I'm not in the right headspace to fix that problem now, so I change into running shorts and a tank top, throw my hair into a ponytail, and find my shoes.

Just as I finish lacing my sneakers, I hear a soft knock on my door. Assuming it's probably a neighbor offering condolences or possibly complaining about the smell—I involuntarily glance over at the still-full trash can, feeling embarrassment coloring my cheeks—I decide to wait until they walk away before heading out, pausing by the door uncertainly.

The knock comes again, louder and more forceful this time. "I know you're in there, Rachel."

My entire body stills, frozen in place.

The pounding noise continues to overwhelm the small space, but I can't force myself to move. "Rachel, I'm sorry. Please. I can explain everything. Please open up."

I haven't heard my sister's voice since the day our mom received her diagnosis four months ago. Yet, I still recognize it instantly. Contemplating ignoring her, I briefly consider pretending to be asleep or not at home.

Another knock, softer this time. "Rachel, please," she pleads, and I can hear the tears she's struggling to hold back.

With a sigh and a lot of hesitation, I reluctantly open the door. Abby pushes it the rest of the way open and throws her arms around me with such force that I stumble backward. Amidst her sobs, all I can make out are mumbled words of "thank god," "I'm so sorry," and "Please." I lean into the hug for about a minute before I can't take anymore. I push her away, folding my arms defensively across my chest.

I should feel relieved to see her, to know she's safe, but all I can muster at this moment is resentment and betrayal.

"What the hell are you doing here?" There is no kindness in my voice, only venom, as I take my sister in.

In the months since I last saw her, Abby's long brown waves have been cut short, barely grazing her shoulders. Her once sharp features now appear gaunt. She's so pale, it's as though she's the one who's been sick, not our mom. Or as if she hasn't seen the sun since she left. It gives her a harsh, angrier appearance, a far cry from the carefree sister I remember growing up with. Her usually bright blue eyes now reflect a dull gray hue, surrounded by redness that suggests she's been crying since the day she left. It's evident she has not been taking care of herself at all.

What I want to ask is, *"Where have you been?"* or *"Are you okay?"* Instead, my anger outweighs my concern when she responds, staring meekly at the floor. "I know I have a lot of explaining to do."

"Damn right, you do." I snap. "That's the least of what you *have to* do. You left me alone. You left Mom alone. You didn't even come to the funeral. Did you even say goodbye to her? Or did you run away and leave her in the dark too?"

I can hear how harsh I sound, but I can't seem to stop myself. There's a part of me that wants to lash out as if to release all the pent-up emotions I've been holding onto these past few months. Yet, a more rational part of me acknowledges that this wouldn't accomplish anything. Abby likely already knows and feels everything I want to scream at her.

"I know," she confirms my thoughts.

Still, I let my irritation win out. "So, what? Now you just knock on my door the day after *I* buried *our* mother and act like everything is okay? Act like she didn't need you? Act like I didn't need you? Well, I did need you, and you weren't here." Abby continues to lock her gaze on the ground, but I can still see the tears pooling in her eyes.

"I know…" her voice trails.

"Is that all you're going to say? You know?" I question, my voice a little bit lighter now that my outburst has concluded. I can feel my anger starting to fade, but hurt begins to take its place.

"That's really all you'll let me say…" she responds, hesitantly. She's staring up at me through her eyelashes now, gauging my reaction before saying anything else.

At that moment, I could see the weight she was carrying. She didn't come here for this. "Look, I'm sorry. You didn't come here to be yelled at."

Her eyes shoot up to meet mine, and a glimmer of hope reflects in the ice blue. "Can we just go somewhere and talk? Maybe the coffee shop we love down the street?" Abby asks.

"You don't want to talk here?" I look around and immediately change my mind. "Never mind. Let me grab my keys."

"I'll drive!" Abby waved her keys excitedly.

Still in my workout clothes, we leave my apartment and make our way to Abby's car.

J's Coffee Connection is within walking distance from where I live. I almost always walk there when I need a coffee fix, but it is one of the hottest days we've had so far this year, and Abby insists on driving. Abby has never been an outdoors person and, as she would put it, hates to sweat. She has always been a petite person, and never had to go to the gym or stay active to keep her figure. She eats whatever she wants and has never had to worry about gaining a pound. She has never been the type to choose salad and water over steak and dessert.

On the other hand, I make a conscious effort to try to walk wherever possible and frequently run the trail behind my apartment. I'm mindful of my diet, usually choosing healthy meals during the week. I always used to joke with Abby about dragging her onto the hiking trail one day, but that has yet to happen.

In these aspects, we are polar opposites. However, in most other aspects of our personalities, we're the same, though Abby tends to be a bit more outgoing than me.

Our true differences come out in our appearances. I look so much like our mom—we both have the same straight, honey-brown hair, dark blue eyes, and porcelain skin tone. Abby, on the other hand, must be the perfect combination of both our parents. She doesn't look like our mom and, from the pictures I've seen of our dad, she doesn't solely resemble him either.

We drive the two minutes to J's Coffee in silence. Abby doesn't even turn on the radio to fill the empty space with noise, a clear sign that she is anxious about something. This, too, is also a trait we share. As soon as she parks the car, she stares at me for a few seconds before saying, "Shall we?" and heading inside.

We walk in past the counter and head straight to our favorite table. There is a little alcove in the back of the coffee shop surrounded by three walls of windows that allow you to look out onto the street. You can people-watch from this spot all day if you want to or, you can simply enjoy the quiet and privacy the little nook provides. It's far enough away from the other tables that you can lose a whole day there getting lost in your own world. It's almost always available whenever Abby and I make our Sunday morning appearance, and I've wondered more than once whether that was intentional by the staff.

Jessie walks over to us with a glowing smile flashing in our direction and starts pouring coffee into the empty cups set on the table. "It's been such a long time since I've seen you girls in here! So sorry to hear about your mama. She was such a wonderful lady."

I haven't been stopping in for anything other than a to-go cup of coffee since my mom was diagnosed, and I couldn't decide if it was because I was busy helping Mom or if it was because I was avoiding coming in without Abby.

"Thanks, Jessie. You know she loved this place. And you," I add with a little too much emotion in my voice. I'm not sure I'm ready to talk about her with anyone just yet.

Abby sits next to me, unmoving and quiet.

"Well, I'll let you girls get settled in. I'll be back with your blueberry muffins in just a minute!" Jessie walks away a little too cheerful. I love Jessie like a second mom, but the emotional contrast with how I'm feeling is almost too much to take. In my mind, everyone who knew my mom should be just as sad as I am right now, including her.

For the first few minutes after Jessie walks away, we stare out the window, one of us occasionally stealing a glance at the other. Abby shrugs off the grey denim jacket she has on, revealing a large tattoo of a bird-looking creature on her left arm right above the long scar she'd had since she was a kid.

"A tattoo? A haircut? Anything else changed in the past few months?"

"It's a Phoenix," is all she says, her voice soft again.

After a few more moments, Abby breaks the silence. "Happy birthday…" She says it hesitantly like she's only acknowledging that it's my birthday because she has no idea what else to say.

How did I forget about my birthday? "Thanks. I didn't even remember it was today." *I guess burying your mother alone will do that to you*, I think to myself cynically.

"How did you forget your own birthday? Don't most people celebrate the whole week? Some girls even give themselves the whole month, and you forgot yours?" She's trying to lighten the mood, but the joke doesn't land for me.

"I don't know, Abigail. Maybe putting my mother in the ground this morning just fucked with my memory a bit." I snap. "Is that a good enough excuse for you? Or should I remind you that the only other person I'd even want to celebrate with was M.I.A for the last four months, up until 20 minutes ago? Are those good enough reasons to maybe not give a shit about turning 25 today?" I somehow manage to not raise my voice, to not draw attention, but I am fuming. My anger is unmistakable to anyone who can see my face or hear the ice in my tone.

Abby flinches but recovers quickly. "I know it's been difficult for you. It hasn't been easy for me either."

"Difficult?" I scoff. "If that isn't an understatement, I don't know what is. But don't sit here and pretend like you know anything about how I feel. You didn't have to take care of Mom, drive her to her appointments, make sure she got all her medications, and watch her die. You didn't have to share her last good moments with her, knowing they were probably her last good moments. You didn't have to grieve alone or plan her funeral alone.

"I didn't know if I was ever going to see you again or where you went. Why? We didn't even get a phone call. Just a text once a month to let us know you were alive. Questioning whether or not it was even you who sent the text. Do you think I never thought about running away, too? You and Mom are the only family I ever had, and you abandoned both of us at the very moment you and I found out we were going to lose her. You abandoned me. Did you even care? Did you even think about us once?

"All that, and then, what? You decided to randomly show up at my door the afternoon after I had to bury her by myself, fake a smile to all those people who didn't know her like we did, who didn't love her like we did. And I can't believe you didn't even show up. Did you even get to say goodbye?"

I stop to catch my breath. When I look up, I see Abby still staring out the window. She doesn't move, and regret bubbles to the surface as I catch the lines on her face where she has let a few tears fall.

"I'm sorry. I'm not trying to make you cry," I say, a little unconvincingly. I don't want to be the cause of any more of her pain, but I meant every word I said. That makes it hard to apologize for my words sincerely, but I should adjust my tone. Part of me has also wondered whether or not she even cares, and the tears confirm that she does. On some level, anyway.

Abby keeps staring, keeps crying, for a few more seconds. I'm starting to hope that Jessie is reading the situation and won't bring our muffins over until all the tears have stopped. "You're right. I don't know," she finally admits.

"Where were you?"

"I just traveled around a bit. I needed to clear my head. I needed to cope."

I laugh, then, not too kindly.

"Cope?" I scoff. "We all needed to cope. Mom needed to come to terms with the fact she was dying, and her youngest daughter had just left her. I needed to deal with the fact that I was losing the only family I ever had all at the same time."

"That was the wrong thing to say," she starts. "But you were never going to lose me. I just needed some time." She continued, as though I was being dramatic. She might as well have rolled her eyes.

"Time? Time for what? I don't understand what feelings you needed to work through that we weren't all trying to work through. That we couldn't all work through together."

Feelings of abandonment were starting to win out over everything else. My anger was rising to the surface fast, and I was losing control of my emotions. Whatever her reasoning, she left without a word when Mom and I needed her. Even though she had come here to talk, she isn't giving me much in the way of information, and it all feels too little too late anyway. About a day too late.

It hits me all at once, how hurt and alone I have been feeling for the past four months, and Abby being here now doesn't fix that. It only makes it worse. I had to do everything alone, and she shows up right after all the hard parts were finished.

Catching the look in my eyes, Abby starts in a rush, "Rachel, look. I can explain everything. I did have a reason, a purpose for everything." She's looking at me, eyes pleading. She knows that I'm about to shut down. She will always know me better than anyone no matter how long we're apart. "Mom told me something right after she was diagnosed. I need to..."

My anger spills out of me, uncontrollably. I jump out of my seat and cut her off. "You know, Mom told me so many things after she was diagnosed. Good things, bad things, everything in between. We had some of our better moments, enjoying what little time we had left together. Not one thing she said made me want to abandon my fucking family."

Grabbing my wallet, I turn toward the door and leave without another word.

She doesn't follow me. I'm not sure if I want her to or not.

Abby drove us to the coffee shop, but I've walked myself back to my apartment from here hundreds of times. Walking will be a good way to clear my head anyway, especially since I never got my run in earlier, but all I can think about is how abandoned I feel.

I'm being selfish, only concerned with how I feel, but I can't come up with a single explanation that would make what Abby did feel okay.

When I get back to the apartment, the first thing I do is call Kara. Kara has been my best friend since kindergarten. She grew up with both Abby and me, and she knows us well enough to be objective when I complain to her. She's also the easiest person to talk to and won't sugarcoat the things I need to hear right now.

She picks up on the first ring. "Rach, what's up? How are you feeling?"

"Funny you should ask. I need to come over. Are you around?"

CHAPTER 2 – APRIL 2002

EVELYN

I imagine I'm drowning. Piercing cries, overwhelming emotions, and sleep deprivation all become physical barriers that I have to fight my way through before I can reach the surface for air. But the swim seems never-ending. My legs are weak, and my arms ache. My best efforts to swim to the surface only leave me in the same place I started. Every time I think I've overcome even the smallest obstacle, something else appears in its place. Eventually, I fear, my lungs will run out of air, my heart will run out of fight, and I will fall to the deepest depths of the ocean where no one will ever find me.

Of course, all of this is in my head. I suffer only mental obstacles, not physical ones. Still, my feet move as though through molasses anyway. A smile takes effort, real effort, spending energy that I don't have to spare. It's difficult to escape the knowledge that any time spent with my girls drains me faster than it should, as though I'm using every effort to keep up a wall for them. To keep them from seeing me broken down while I work through emotions I don't understand. Emotions I don't have a solid grasp on. Emotions that aren't their fault.

I stand in my kitchen, a ritual I follow most mornings, gazing out the window at our small backyard garden. It's the perfect time of year for daydreaming, for losing oneself in all the beauty that nature offers. The weather is warming, but the infamous

Florida humidity has yet to fill the air. Nature's own springtime rejuvenation brings new life to the backyard, and the world regains its color, its vitality. Perhaps the same will happen for me.

Presently, I find myself daydreaming about being able to escape into my little garden, my safe haven. I could recoup there for a while, come back refreshed, and be the mother I need to be.

Gazing at my beautiful, three-week-old daughter, I summon a smile, though it feels like a feat of endurance, because I know she deserves nothing less. I still find it hard to believe that Scott and I brought another little miracle into the world. Despite the way I've been feeling, I recognize Rachel and Abigail for the miracles they are. They fill a void I never knew existed. I would be lost without them, and I don't know what I ever did before them. Witnessing Rachel's care for her newborn sister makes everything I'm feeling worth it. I know, above all else, Scott and I would do anything to protect them.

Scott walks into the kitchen and wraps me in a hug from behind. "You look absolutely beautiful this morning, Evelyn." He reaches his head over my shoulder to kiss me on the cheek.

As I turn around, I find him impeccably dressed in one of his finest suits. He has on my favorite light blue tie, the one that brings out his eyes. It brightens the dark blue I so often get lost in. Those deep blue eyes, reminiscent of the ocean depths, that he seems to have passed onto both of our daughters. I can't help but compare his polished appearance to my current state – clad in a nightgown that has seen better days, which I have been wearing for three days straight, adorned with a baby spit-up and slobber. With a playful roll of my eyes, I dismiss his compliment.

"I thought you didn't have to work today. It's Saturday," I complain. The whine I hear in my voice makes me cringe, but I can't seem to help it.

"I know, sweetheart. I have to make sure all of my clients are back in order given that I was out of the office the past few weeks. I won't be more than a few hours today. If you need anything at all, just call. I'll come straight home."

"Alright." He knows I won't disrupt his work, not when he spent the last few weeks home with me in the midst of working toward a big promotion. He cares about his work too much, but he cares about me more. I won't ask him to choose. Not when he's supporting all four of us.

"I love you, Evey." He kisses the top of my forehead as I close my eyes and lean into him. He bends down to kiss Abigail on her forehead, too.

"Hey, Evelyn?" Scott starts with a mischievous look in his eye as he stands upright again.

"Yes, dear?" I play along.

"Have you seen a little girl around? She would be around this high?" He motions to his knees. "Almost three, beautiful long brown hair, favorite color is pink?"

"It's PURPLE!!" a tiny, animated, voice shouts from the kitchen pantry. Rachel jumps out and runs to wrap her dad in a hug.

"Oh! Silly me! How could I forget?" Scott jokingly slapped his forehead. Kneeling next to Rachel, Scott explains, "Listen, Daddy needs to go to work for a little bit. Can I trust you to take care of mommy and baby Abby while I'm gone?"

"Yes! Yes! I'm the big sister!" Rachel jumps around enthusiastically, her endless energy on full display. My little caretaker already. Ever since Abigail was born, Rachel took on the role of "big girl" with so much pride, and it was one of the greatest things to watch her succeed in it.

"Excellent! They'll be in good hands then. Love you, bubba."

"Love you, Daddy!"

"Love you, Scott! Don't be too late, okay?"

He leans in for one more kiss before grabbing his briefcase from the kitchen table and heading out the door.

It doesn't take long for that feeling to settle back in. Scott has a way of making the hopelessness disappear. Maybe that is because he takes some of the pressure off me, even if it's only temporary. As soon as he leaves, chaos ensues. All I can see are the dirty dishes piling up in the sink. Rachel is hungry again but also wants to play with her toys. Abigail, who had slept through most of the morning, decides to wake up at that exact moment and is probably hungry, too.

This week is Scott's first week back at work, and, without him here, this all feels overwhelming. What I want is to close Rachel and Abigail in their rooms and go back to sleep until he got home.

Stop. You can't think like that. Stop.

I shake my head at my own intrusive thoughts, as though trying to shake a physical object out of my head.

Having a child is hard. I know that. Having two children is harder. I know that, too. I love my children beyond any real measure. I have always dreamed of having the life, the husband, the children I do now. After Scott and I had Rachel, we wanted another right away. It took some time, but Abigail came along almost 3 years later.

I had a difficult time adjusting to motherhood when we had Rachel, as anyone would I suppose, but I absolutely adored her. Our whole life became about her, and we couldn't have been any happier. Scott always talked about wanting boys, but Rachel had him wrapped around her finger in no time at all. Naturally, Abby did, too.

I began staying home more often after having Rachel. None of our friends had children, so they didn't understand all of the inconveniences that came with scheduling things around them. I didn't work anymore – I didn't need to in the first place, and we decided that Scott's income was more than enough to support the three of us. This way I could stay home with the baby. At first, I barely noticed everything I was missing out on because I was so tired all the time. Rachel was taking up all my mental and physical energy.

It's been a little different since Abigail. It feels harder. It feels mentally and physically exhausting in a way I've never felt before. I don't feel as connected to Abigail, and I'm even feeling less connected to Rachel than I did before, but the doctors tell me that will pass. I just keep telling myself I have to make it through the hours that I'm here by myself, and everything will be alright as soon as Scott gets home.

It's not a way to live, but it's temporary.

After the girls wake up from their naps, Rachel is more rambunctious than usual, and Abigail doesn't allow me to stand still. I turn to my almost-three-year-old to come up with a game plan, a clear sign of desperation on my part. I am feeling the decision fatigue setting in already, and it is only 11 in the morning.

"Rach, sweetie, what do you want to do today?"

"Animals! Animals!" she shouts, jumping around the living room mimicking kangaroo.

"Okay, do you want to see water animals or land animals?"

"Kitty cat! Big, giant kitty cat!"

Alright, zoo it is. I dress Rachel in shorts and a t-shirt that has "Future Zookeeper" written on the front with pictures of a glitter-covered lion, tiger, and cheetah – all the big cats that seem to be her favorite today.

I walk her back to the living room and take out a few toys out for her to play with while I get Abigail ready to go. I change Abigail's diaper and get her in a giraffe print onesie I got as part of an "animal prints" pack Rachel picked out the last time we visited the zoo. She does love her animals.

When I walk back out to the living room, Rachel isn't there.

"Rachel?" I call out, but there's no response. Panic sets in. I check in the pantry she was hiding in earlier, then behind the couch, and in the closet by the front door. After searching everywhere I can think of in the main part of the house, I call Rachel's name more frantically.

"Rach, baby, this isn't funny. Mommy needs to know where you are!"

Nothing.

I am standing in the kitchen when I see the side door closed. The door leads down a narrow hallway to our laundry room which sits separate from the rest of the house. A major design flaw or a poorly thought-out addition to the house, the walls are very thin and don't match the rest of the structure. The humidity sometimes causes the door to expand and get stuck, which is why we typically leave it open.

I run over to the closed door and wriggle it until it opens. I find Rachel on the floor, silently crying. "Rach, what's wrong?"

"The door got stuck," she explains between sobs.

"Sweetie, that's okay. You're okay. Mommy will never let you stay stuck if you get stuck."

"You yelled," she accuses me, still talking through tears and shallow breaths.

"I was just worried. I couldn't find you, that's all. You're okay."

She wipes her tears as she nods her head.

"We have to be careful about closing these doors from now on, okay? You're okay." I wrap her in a hug until her tears stop flowing.

"Okay, Mommy. I'm sorry."

"It's alright." I stand up to get her a tissue, and she walks back into the kitchen holding my hand. "Do you still want to go to the zoo to see the big cats?"

"Big kitty cats! Big kitty cats!" I laugh as she starts jumping around like a kangaroo again. This is the fastest I have seen her tears turn to laughter in a long time.

I leave a note for Scott to let him know where we would be and when we would be home, and then Rachel and I laugh all the way to the car as she pretends to be every animal she can think of. She practices her animal noises for Abigail even though her little sister stays sound asleep the whole way to the zoo.

The moments filled with joy, even the ones that come after tears, always remind me why I love being a mother. They pull me out of my sadness, even if just for a moment.

When we return home from the zoo, I notice the note I left for Scott still sitting untouched on the table. He hasn't been home yet. I try not to let it bother me, but the disappointment sits heavily in my chest.

I will call him if he isn't home after I finish getting the girls their dinner. In the meantime, I move a few of Rachel's toys from the living room to the kitchen floor and pull Abigail's bassinet so it is next to the kitchen table – far enough away from the stove so that I'm comfortable nothing will spill or splash on her but close enough that I can see her if she starts to fuss.

I work on cooking my specialty – Kraft Mac and Cheese. As with any situation where a mother tries to do everything on her own, I manage this successfully for just under two minutes before Rachel starts playing a little too loudly, banging her plastic blocks on the tile floor. This, in turn, wakes Abigail from her afternoon nap.

I am immediately overstimulated by the noise, now made worse with Abigail crying, and I yell at Rachel to calm down while not exhibiting any signs of calm myself. Rachel starts screaming while I try to soothe Abigail, and the water starts boiling over on the stove. I yell at Rachel again to move from the stove, and the face she gave me, like a wounded puppy, breaks my heart.

You're failing. You're failing.

What am I doing? How can I not even get through a dinner that takes less than 10 minutes to prepare?

Rachel runs into the living room where I can still see her, and I begin to run after her until I remember the stove is still on. I had only boiled the water and hadn't started actually cooking anything yet, so I'm able to turn the stove off and then try to console Rachel.

Through sobs, Rachel says, "You're yelling a lot today, Mommy."

"I know, sweetie. I don't mean to yell so much. I don't want you playing so close to the stove. You could've gotten hurt, and I was scared." I shake my head, still feeling overwhelmed but knowing I have to finish dinner. I don't have the energy for the crying, the conversation, anything. "If I let you play in here, will you be careful?"

Rachel nods her head enthusiastically, like I had just bestowed upon her a special privilege.

"Okay, and will you watch out for your sister for me? She fell back asleep, and maybe it'll be quieter in here for her. Can you do that for me?" Again, she nods. Why didn't I just do this from the start?

"Just be careful, alright? I'll be right in there if you need anything," I explain, pointing back toward the kitchen. I stand up and am almost back to the stove when Rachel stops me.

"Mommy?"

"Yes, sweetie?"

"Does this make me a big girl?"

I laugh. "Of course, it does! Only big girls get to play in the living room while mommies are cooking dinner!"

"Yay! Big Girl! I'm a Big Girl!" she starts dancing.

I put my finger to my lips to indicate she needs to dance a little quieter, and she starts doing her "Big Girl" chant in a whisper while she dances around the living room.

Two hours later, I am finishing up putting the girls to bed when I hear the front door open, and Scott walks in. I greet him while he is still at the door, and the smell of alcohol on his breath immediately kills my already fragile mood. He doesn't seem to notice as he wraps me in a hug.

"How was your day?"

"Long and exhausting. You? How was work?"

"Oh, it was busy. Much busier than I had anticipated. The guys wanted to take me out for a little celebration for my first week back. I know I should've called, but I wasn't expecting to be out so late."

He walks into the living room, and I follow, letting my face fall only when he can no longer see it.

"Where are the girls?" He asks, looking around disappointedly. "They're asleep already?"

"Yes, dear. It *is* late."

"You truly do everything." He takes my face in his hands and gently kisses my forehead. I struggle not to roll my eyes before he starts toward the bedroom. "I'm going to take a quick shower," he tells me as he closes the bedroom door behind him.

I wait on the couch, TV on for some background noise, as minutes pass. Then a half hour. Then a full hour. Scott is still showering or getting himself ready for bed or whatever it is he feels the need to do besides spend time with me.

I understand his need to work, but it *is* Saturday. I spent the whole day without one bit of help, and he spent the whole day missing how quickly Rachel learns now, how she can name all the animals at the zoo, how she calls Abigail "her baby," and how protective she is of her. He doesn't see how much she's grown in the last few weeks. And despite missing all of that, despite telling me that he knows I do everything, I sometimes don't believe he even knows what that means or how "doing stuff" isn't the only thing he needs to be home for.

I also realize that I *am* overwhelmed by things that shouldn't overwhelm me. I am tired, I am sad, and I am angrier than usual. I have been yelling at Rachel far more than she's ever experienced from me. He doesn't see that either.

He's been back at work for a week now, and he's already falling back into old patterns: long days, late nights, working weekends, and drinking at the end of every day. I don't know if it bothers me more because there are two girls now, or if I just need my husband to be here for me right now in a way I didn't before. I don't know how to tell him any of that without destroying the image he has of me as the perfect mother and wife. He would never understand.

Still, he's my husband, and he has always been supportive of my every need. He has never truly given me a reason to doubt that he wouldn't understand or take care of me in a situation like this.

Yet, I feel more of myself breaking as I wait for him to join me on the couch.

It has been well over an hour when I look at the clock again. At this point, it's time for me to get some sleep since I know this will be the only chance I get for the night. Scott should be home tomorrow, and we can spend time together then.

When I walk into the bedroom, I find Scott not even showered, fully clothed, passed out on top of the covers. Doing my best not to wake him, I climb into bed, turn the lights out, and try to hold back my tears as I fall asleep.

CHAPTER 3 – JUNE 2024

RACHEL

"So, you're telling me she just showed up out of nowhere? After your mom's funeral? Not even a text?"

I nod my head. I am curled up under a blanket, my chin resting on my knees with a cup of hot tea in my hands. As soon as I got off the phone with Kara, I drove straight to her house, resisting the urge to run every red light.

Kara and I have been best friends since kindergarten. She stole my markers, and I hit her for it. We were both put in timeout where we couldn't stop making each other laugh despite our laughter getting us in even more trouble. She was the first friend I made after moving to Bradenton, and we've been inseparable ever since. We had classes together almost every year after that, ran track together in middle school, and even lived on the same street for a while. We have never even had a real fight.

Growing up together means she knows Abby well, too. She was the only person I could think of to call, the only person I wanted to talk to who would understand everything I needed to say. As soon as I walk through her front door, I break down. She hugs me for as long as I need, before setting me up with a cup of hot tea and a box of tissues.

"That's fucked up."

"Tell me about it."

"That just doesn't sound like the Abby we know and love, you know? For her to take off right after your mom's diagnosis seems insanely out of character, but we've judged that decision enough already. To not even come back for the funeral this morning and then to show up at your apartment after, unannounced, with a bullshit explanation… I don't even have words for that." Kara shakes her head in disbelief as if trying to figure out a way to make it make sense.

"Yeah, well, she did," I reply with an icy tone. Not because of Kara, though. She is right – none of this is like Abby. We have all been so close our whole lives, especially since we've always been all each other has had. Maybe that's why it hurts so much that she left and then came back the way she did.

I know Kara is still hurting over the fact that Abby didn't say anything to her before leaving either, but she would never admit that to me.

"I know, I know," she backtracks. "But there must have been a reason, right? 'I was having trouble coping, so I abandoned my whole family' seems extra shitty and, quite frankly, not that believable."

"That's what I've been trying to figure out for months now."

"Did she say anything the day she left? Was she acting weird?"

"Haven't we already gone over all of this?" Annoyance is still the main emotion forcing my tone.

"I know. Just humor me. Walk me through 'diagnosis day,' and then walk me through today. Maybe something she said today will cause something from back then to stand out?"

"If you say so," I start reluctantly. 'Diagnosis day,' as we begrudgingly refer to it now, is not my favorite memory to recall. "We were both at the hospital with mom when she got the results of all the testing they were doing. Obviously, all three of us took the diagnosis pretty hard, but we spent most of the rest of the day together. That's all Mom wanted.

"So, we spent a couple of hours with her talking, playing cards, whatever. Mom eventually got hungry, complaining that the food she got at the hospital sucked. Hospital food always sucks. She asked me to run down to the cafeteria to get us all something to eat. I was only gone maybe thirty minutes. I had trouble finding the cafeteria at first, and when I got there, the place was packed. Mom wanted some special sandwich... That detail obviously doesn't matter. Anyway, when I got back, Abby was gone, and my mom was acting strange. I assumed they just fought about something. We all knew my mom was going to start treatment. Abby wanted her to enjoy the time she had left rather than suffer through her last few months. In her mind, it wasn't worth the extra few weeks she might get at best. Honestly, I felt the same, but my mom said any extra time she got with us was worth any suffering caused by treatment. Abby hated that, and she was way more vocal about it than I was." I pause then, giving myself a chance to catch my breath.

"All my mom said to me was that Abby had to leave, and her tone didn't leave any room for further discussion. We didn't say anything else about her for the rest of the night. I called Abby the next morning, but she ignored all of my calls. Two days later, I got a text from her saying she was 'traveling.' She said she needed to clear her head and that she'd check in when she could. Whatever the hell that means. I asked Mom if Abby had spoken to her since she left the hospital, and she only shook her head. She was messed up for weeks.

"I did ask her once if this had anything to do with that day in the hospital and she got so mad at me. She told me Abby had her reasons, and basically told me to mind my business. It was such a weird reaction for Mom, too, but I still assumed she didn't want the constant reminders that Abby was gone. We got her first 'check-in' text, about a month later. *'I'm doing okay.'* That's all it said.

I can hear the volume of my voice steadily rising, and I'm talking more animatedly, using my hands more, as I get more emotional.

"Every time I argued with my mom about just reporting her missing, she told me, *no*. She argued that the police would only say that her text messages were proof that she was not missing. I gave her every argument in the book – What if it's not her texting? What if something is wrong, and she doesn't want us to know or worry? Mom always said to let her do what she needs to for herself right now, and Abby would come back when she's ready. When she's ready for what?" I scoff, still not understanding. "As though it wasn't hard on all three of us, and Abby didn't just abandon her family. Somehow, I just felt out of the loop. It felt like even Mom was being too calm about the whole thing."

Out of breath now, I meet Kara's gaze and shrug, letting her know that's all I have.

"Maybe she just didn't want to spend the rest of her time arguing with you about Abby or fighting with Abby about coming home?" Kara offers as a solution.

I realize I had let another tear escape during my monologue; I wipe it away swiftly. Feeling all the sadness that my mom felt, all the anger and loss I feel, is overwhelming. Kara hands me a tissue and looks at me hesitantly, waiting for me to give her some kind of sign that I'm okay. I blow my nose and shrug my shoulders again.

Kara takes it for what it is – a silent confirmation to continue.

"Okay, now today."

"Today, I don't know. She just showed up. I didn't even know if I was going to let her in. She kept knocking, and she sounded desperate. Desperate for what? I don't know, but she kept knocking. She kept apologizing, so I let her in.

"She only made excuses though. *It's been difficult for her, too. She had her reasons. Mom told her something, and it was significant enough to make her run away. Somehow, I just wouldn't understand.*" Sarcasm is seeping through my words. "At least that's what it all felt like. I don't know where she gets off telling me that it was hard for her when she doesn't even know what I've had to go through without her the last few months. She doesn't understand."

Kara senses my anger growing and tries to reel me back in. "That was a shitty thing for her to say. But she did leave, and maybe she doesn't understand how hard it was for you to be here alone taking care of your mom. She should understand, but maybe she's been to wrapped up in her own reasons and she can't. Either way, I get where you're coming from. She's never been the self-involved type, so what's her deal now?"

"Exactly," I agree. "She acts as though Mom's diagnosis wasn't hard on all of us. On mom, who had to come to terms with the fact she was leaving her daughters without a mother. On me, who was also about to lose a mom and who had to be the one to watch her die. This was hard on all of us, not just Abby. We've never been apart for more than a few days, the three of us, and not even a phone call? It just doesn't make sense."

"You just mentioned a conversation that changed something for her."

"Yes…?"

"And at the hospital, you left for half an hour, and Abby was gone?"

"Yes, again. Where are you going with this?" I motion for her to get to the point.

"And that was when you stopped hearing from her? When she basically disappeared?"

"What's your point?" I say out loud now. "I told you that was probably a fight about treatments or something. She wasn't getting her way, and they argued."

"Well, maybe. But she wouldn't run away over a conversation about your mom's treatment, right? Especially if she was arguing to have better quality time with your mom? It doesn't make sense that she would rather have no time with your mom. Could she have told Abby anything else that would set her off like this? Maybe make her want to get away?"

"No, Kara." I fight the urge to roll my eyes but feel the sarcasm seeping back into my tone anyway. "There is nothing that I can come up with that could be said in 20 minutes that would cause that reaction from Abby. There is no bombshell hidden family secret that would make her run off. It's always just been the three of us, and we've always been so open about everything. You know that."

"Okay, you're right. That's a little far-fetched. But something did make her run off. You have to talk to her. You have to give her a chance to explain." Kara gives me a *'you know I'm right'* look that I can't quite force myself to give into just yet.

"Even if my mom did do something to piss her off or did confess some scary family secret…" I pause to roll my eyes, unable to hold back this time… "nothing would be bad enough to leave Mom alone through all of this… to leave me!" My voice breaks on the last word, and I know I sound like a stubborn, wounded child.

Until now, I have only let a tear or two escape, and have managed to hold back the full-on waterworks. All the emotions I've bottled up over the past four months are threatening to spill out. Cracks are forming in the dam that I've built, and the tears start flowing. I can't control them anymore.

Kara hugs me again and brings the box of tissues closer to me. As she's rubbing her hands up and down my back, she says, gently, "Rachel, you have to talk to her. I'm sure there is some kind of semi-reasonable explanation. She's your sister. And if there isn't, then you just come back here and bitch some more."

I crack a hint of a smile at the last part. "You're right."

"It's what I'm here for."

"But tomorrow. I'm still too heated, and I wouldn't give her a fair chance right now. I'll sleep on it and call her in the morning."

Kara nods in agreement, and we both know that the conversation is over for the time being.

The next morning, I jolt awake to the blaring sound of Kara's alarm. We ended up staying awake and talking almost the whole night, gossiping and chatting about everything under the sun while old Shirley Temple movies we used to love played in the background. It turned out to be exactly the kind of night I needed, like we were teenagers having a sleepover again. For a little while, I got to escape reality with my best friend.

Unfortunately, reality hits hard as I look up to read 7 A.M. on the alarm clock. I barely move my arm an inch, reaching to shut it off, when Kara rushes into the room. "I'm sorry. I'm so sorry," she mumbles. "I usually wake up before the alarm, but I don't shut it off. I like it to go off when I need to start getting ready. I didn't even think about it this morning."

"You wake up *before* 7 A.M.? On purpose?" I grumble.

"You know I've always been an early riser. Do you want coffee?" She grins at me sheepishly.

"Is the sky blue?" I ask.

"One cup, coming right up!" She does her best impersonation of an old English butler as she walks back out into the kitchen.

I force myself to trudge out to Kara's living room. She has a nice apartment, a little bigger than mine. At least she has a bedroom with a door. I walk over to the couch where we spent most of the night talking and sit down, sighing.

"Here you go." Kara hands me my mug, and the smell of vanilla has me immediately perking up. "No sighing before the day has even started. I have to go get ready for work. Are you going to be alright?"

"Yeah, don't worry about me. I'll wake up with the coffee and then head out!"

"Are you going to call Abby today?"

"I will once I'm on my way home. I think," I add, noncommittally.

Kara gives me a look that lets me know she's not all that convinced, then walks back into her bedroom. She comes out 10 minutes later, ready to go.

"Don't be afraid to call me today. I'm available, whatever you need. Let me know how it goes either way. Love you!" I stand to give her one more hug, and then she heads out the door.

As soon as Kara leaves, I sit back down on her couch, coffee in hand. I am not quite ready to head back to my apartment yet. Part of me doesn't particularly want to relive the memory of Abby showing up the way she did. Another part of me feels like going back to my apartment means officially getting back to normal life, and I am not ready for that either. My mind drifts to the mess waiting for me, and I can't help the shudder that follows.

All the anger I felt yesterday helps me push aside the sadness and pain that comes along with the events of the last 48 hours. Burying my mom on my own. Just burying her, period. Even knowing it was inevitable didn't seem to make it easier. And now, facing all that still needs to be done feels overwhelming.

My job was gracious enough to give me time off the past few weeks. Normally, I work from home and as part of a marketing team for a nearby hospital. They aren't drowning without me. I worked when I could over the past few months, but I didn't stick to your typical 9-to-5 schedule. I mostly worked while my mom was sleeping or in the lobby of her chemo appointments.

After she passed, though, I told work I would need a few weeks off for funeral planning and going through all my mom's things. I thought I would be cleaning out her house and settling everything alone, but maybe Abby will help now that she's back.

Ugh. Abby. I know I have to call her. Even if it's only to see if she'll be around to help clear out Mom's house this week. That can be my excuse. I need her. I can work through the emotional task of getting my sister back, or at least finding out why she left, when the timing is a bit better. I will call her today, but not until I've had another cup of coffee. And maybe after I watch a feel-good movie or two.

I stand up and stretch my whole body out before making my way back into the kitchen. Kara has one of those single-serve coffee makers, but I notice a whole pot of coffee next to it and a note on the counter.

I knew you'd need more than one cup to muster up the energy for tackling today. Let me know if you need anything! Call Abby!!!

Instead of writing her name, she signs the note with a heart. I smile at how well she knows me, pour my coffee, and make my way back to the couch. After scrolling through every streaming service for what felt like forever — again — I land on an old favorite *How to Lose a Guy in 10 Days.* I grab the box of tissues from the coffee table knowing full well I have a tendency to ugly-cry at happy endings. I curl up with a blanket and my coffee and sink into the couch.

I wake up sometime later, groggy and disoriented. The clock on what I now remember is Kara's stove shows 11 A.M. I startle as I realize I am holding a big cup of coffee. Some part of me must have realized I was dozing off, because I find the coffee mug, still full, on the coffee table in front of me. The sun streams through the kitchen window, and the street outside is bustling with noise, a stark contrast compared to just a few hours ago. The change in atmosphere in only a few short hours makes me wish I had the discipline to pull myself out of bed every morning as early as Kara does so that I could enjoy the more peaceful hours of the day.

I laugh at myself for even thinking that. What a pipe dream that is.

With a groan and another full-body stretch, I get up and head back to Kara's bedroom. I hadn't planned on spending the night anywhere but my apartment last night, so I hadn't brought a change of clothes or anything else I need this morning. I need to change out of the sweatpants and T-shirt I borrowed from Kara and back into yesterday's clothes. In the bathroom, I splash water on my face and use the mouthwash I find on her counter. My hair is unmanageable, so I pull it up into a messy bun.

Before I head out for the day, I fold the blankets on the couch, wash my coffee cup, and leave a note under hers.

Thank you for everything! As always, you're the best!

I sign my note with a heart, too.

It's a 30-minute drive from Kara's apartment to mine, so I had plenty of time to talk myself into and out of calling Abby about ten times before finally deciding to just make the call. After a few rings, the call goes to voicemail. Relief floods over me for a moment before I scold myself. What I should do is call again to let her know I'm serious about talking. She might think I'm only calling to argue and refuse to pick up out of principle.

It rings and then goes to voicemail again.

Frustrated, I throw my phone onto the passenger seat. Where does she get off not wanting to talk to me right now? I remind myself that she could be busy with something and that I should give her some time to call back. Abby was always better at giving people the benefit of the doubt, so I try to keep her voice in my head as I work to stay calm.

I am almost home now, but I still need more caffeine – spoken (*or thought*) like a true caffeine junkie – so I stop at J's Coffee again. I catch Jessie's eye as soon as I step through the front door, and she runs over to the counter to take care of me.

"The usual?"

"Yes, please." I pull out my wallet to hand her a $5 bill.

"On me, dear," she says, shaking her head and shooting me a look that lets me know there is no room for argument.

"Oh, Jessie. You don't have to do that."

"I do, sweetie. I want to." She looks at me with sadness, but not pity. I appreciate that, at least. I've had enough pity the past few weeks to last a lifetime.

A minute later, she walks back with my coffee in a to-go cup. Of course, she remembers that I don't stay unless I have Abby or my mom with me. "Thank you so much. And I'm sorry about everything yesterday. For how I left."

"Not another word," she says firmly, raising a hand to dismiss my concerns as she walks around the counter. When she reaches me, she wraps me in one of those hugs that feel like a shield, like a mother offering all the protection you need. I cherish those hugs, and she always knows exactly when to give them. "You've been through so much, sweetie. Too much. You and Abby will find your way back to each other. You always do. And you need each other now more than ever. Emotions are running high, but it won't always be like this," she says with such certainty that I almost believe her.

"Did she say anything to you?" I need to know.

"No. She stayed for another minute or two before she grabbed her things and left."

My eyes begin to water, but I hold back the tears. I have shed enough already, and I refuse to let myself appear like a complete mess every time I step out in public.

"Just in case," she nods toward a napkin in her outstretched arm. "You know I'm only a block away. I have your caffeine fix ready to go whenever you need it."

I give her a quick nod as I tuck the napkin into my pocket. "Love you, Jessie." I wrap my arms around her in a tight, quick hug and then head back to my car.

I didn't come here for almost 3 weeks when Abby first ran away. This place was ours, and it hurt too much to come back. When I finally returned, a part of me hoped to find Abby sitting at our table in the back, lost in a book or doing a crossword puzzle.

My disappointment must have been obvious because Jessie hurried over to ask what was wrong. Or maybe it was my prolonged absence that tipped her off. Whatever the case, she got my coffee ready and joined me at a table – not the one in the back that I couldn't bear to sit at. We talked for hours as I poured everything out to her about my mom's diagnosis and Abby's disappearance.

After that, I started coming in every day for coffee, except for this past week. Jessie always had my coffee ready, but I never stayed. Not until yesterday. Even so, being there usually made me feel better, even if I only stayed for a few minutes. Ever since Abby and I began showing up weekly, everyone there felt like a second family – especially Jessie. It was one of the most comfortable places for us to just be.

I settle back into my car and head home, holding back tears the entire way.

By the time I arrive home, Abby still hasn't called or texted. I had hoped I might have missed her call while at the coffee shop. I don't want to risk annoying her further, considering she might still be upset with me for storming out on her yesterday. So, I'll wait until later tonight before reaching out again.

In the meantime, I redirect my focus to restoring normalcy as much as possible. I step through the front door of the disaster I am currently calling my apartment for the second time in two days letting out a loud sigh as I take in the chaos around me. I idly wonder why the place didn't magically tidy itself up between yesterday and now.

I pass through the cluttered kitchen, navigate through the mess in my living room, and head straight for the bathroom. Before I can tackle cleaning the entire apartment, I desperately need to shower and change out of my dirty clothes. Once I wash away yesterday's tears and makeup, tie my clean hair into a ponytail, and slip into my "cleaning sweats" and an old t-shirt, I gear up for the daunting task ahead. Loud, wall-thumping music serves as my soundtrack, sure to annoy the neighbors but providing a necessary boost of energy and motivation.

After a few hours, the apartment is finally back to normal. The trash is emptied, the counters are sparkling clean, everything is dusted, and the laundry is washed and neatly folded. I even scrubbed all the floors. Sighing with satisfaction, I collapse onto the couch, order a pizza, and put on the movie I slept through this morning, eager for my dinner to arrive.

Now, the only thing left to clean up is whatever this mess is with my sister.

When I see how late it's gotten and realize Abby still hasn't called back, I decide to send her a text instead of calling again. Maybe she's not answering because she's worried I might yell again. I want to reassure her I don't want to fight. After typing and retyping several times, I finally settle on a short, direct message and hit send.

I'm sorry for everything. I just want to talk. Please call me back. I love you!

A few minutes later, a knock on my door signals the arrival of the pizza. I pay the delivery driver, head into the kitchen to pour myself a glass of my favorite peach wine, and then plop back down onto the couch. I finish my dinner and get about halfway through the movie before I allow myself to check my phone again. Still Nothing.

By the time the movie ends, I still haven't heard anything from her. I start to debate whether I should be worried but decide she probably just needs some space. After how I acted yesterday, giving her some time seems like the right thing to do.

A quick glance at the clock has me wondering where the day went. Planning to be up early the next morning, I decide to call it a night. As I walk to my bed, I do my best to convince myself that Abby is perfectly fine and that we will talk in the morning.

When I wake up the next morning, I am instantly on edge. Today is the day I promised myself I would start packing up my mom's things. Without a deadline, I know I'll keep putting it off, and that's not an option. I grab my phone from the end table next to my bed and see zero notifications. Still nothing from Abby. The pit in my stomach that started forming last night grows.

I climb out of bed and start my typical morning routine, hoping to trick my mind and body into feeling normal. I make my coffee, throw on a pair of leggings and my sneakers, and head out for a run on the trail behind my apartment. I always hated running competitively; it was just something to do when I was younger and Kara was on the team with me. But running like this has always been the perfect escape from reality. My mind focuses only on my heartbeat and the scenery around me.

Unfortunately, it doesn't seem to be doing the trick for me today, so I cut the run short. When I get back, I shower and throw on jeans and another old T-shirt since I know I'll be getting sweaty and dirty later. It occurs to me that maybe going through Mom's things would be something that would get Abby's attention.

I give her another call, but it goes straight to voicemail this time.

Weird.

I leave her a voicemail, hoping it'll get to her somehow. "Hey, Abby. Look, I'm so sorry about the other day. I was on edge, but that's no excuse. I just want to talk, and I promise not to yell or storm out this time. I'm going to mom's house. There's a lot to clean out, and I could use the help. If you get this, and you aren't doing anything, stop over? We can talk there. Okay, that's all I wanted to say. Love you!"

I hang up and stare at my phone for a while. All I can do at this point is hope she shows up. I drive to my mom's house in silence. It's not a long drive – she lived only ten minutes from my apartment – but it's still a clear sign of unmanaged anxiety for me.

My mind races back and forth between worry and annoyance, and the racing thoughts are only made worse with the radio on, so I drive in silence.

Logically, I can't wrap my head around why I'm so worried. Maybe it's a gut feeling, but I have no real proof that anything is wrong. Didn't she just disappear for months without a single word? She didn't respond to my calls or texts then either. But she had sounded so desperate to talk to me yesterday. Had I upset her so much that she went back into hiding? Shouldn't she have expected my reaction at least a little?

My worry shifts to annoyance as I imagine her ignoring my calls because of hurt feelings. As terrible as I was to her, I have every right to feel the way I do. Sure, I could've handled it better, but her shutting me out now is childish and unfair. She had to understand I just needed some time, and seeing her out of the blue like that after months was a shock. At the very least, we both deserve the chance to explain. One bad moment does not mean I wouldn't have given her that opportunity. Throughout all our years together, she has never done anything like this before.

I'm not sure what to think, how to feel, but I do know I'm overthinking everything. I need a distraction. Cleaning and sorting through nearly twenty years of belongings and paperwork could either be the best distraction or a terrible one.

When I pull up to the house Abby and I grew up in, I sit in my car and gaze out the window toward the place that will always be my home. I study the two-story, red brick structure, trying to commit every detail to memory.

There isn't much to it. The one-car driveway is made up of cracked, jagged concrete tiles, and an uneven sidewalk leads up to a dark plum-colored door. The door matches the curtains still hanging in all the front-facing windows.

Mom always insisted that your personality should shine through both the inside and outside of your house if you truly wanted it to feel like a home. I used to think that applied mainly to things like Christmas decorations and lawn care, but for her, it meant a lot of purple. According to her, purple was my first favorite color. She was so dedicated to the things we loved, to what brought us joy, that they became a part of her personality too. Apparently, purple was one of those things that stuck.

I can still picture her garden in the backyard, meticulously organized with separate sections for vegetables and rows of vibrant flowers. There was even a mango tree for a few years when I was younger. But up front, she kept it simple with a few rose bushes lining the front of the house. Our neighbor Glenn, bless his heart, was never the best landscaper, but he always tried to help maintain those bushes whenever he cut Mom's grass. Looking at them now, I can't help but notice that they are starting to look overgrown, as though he hasn't done any of that in weeks. It's almost as if time stopped for him, too, when she took a turn for the worse.

I shrug my shoulders, a small gesture of either resignation or acceptance. Mom probably told him to stop fussing over the yard.

After a few moments, I step out of my car and start towards the door, only to hear a familiar voice call out, "Rachel!"

"Hi, Glenn!" I turn to see my old neighbor standing in his yard, watering his own garden. Glenn, in his late 50s like my mom, moved in next door about a year before we did. His wife Betty, and Mom instantly became best friends. Glenn and Betty never had any kids of their own, but they were always the best babysitters whenever Mom needed help. Betty passed away two years ago, and the two neighbors have only gotten closer since then. My mom never remarried, and Glenn rarely left the house to grocery shop, let alone date, so they kept each other company when their houses got too quiet.

They were always the best of friends, but I never had the courage to pry into their relationship or ask if there was anything more. Not even at the end when we were talking about everything else. It occurs to me to worry about Glenn now that he has lost Evelyn, too.

"How are you doing, Rach?" He puts down the hose he is holding and walks over to give me a hug. I've been getting a lot of those lately.

"I'm doing okay. How are you holding up?"

"One day at a time, that's all I can manage right now." He shakes his head, looking defeated. I force myself to keep the pity out of my gaze, reminding myself how that has made me feel all week.

"I'm going through all of Mom's things. I have some time to clear everything out, but if there is anything you want, just let me know, okay?"

"Thank you. And you let me know if there is anything I can do to help."

"Will do." I give him a soft smile, a half-hearted nod, and then turn to head towards the house.

"Hey Rachel!" he calls as I reach the front door. "Have you heard anything from Abigail?"

I startle, but I manage to compose myself before responding. Why would he be asking about Abigail? "No, I haven't." the lie slips out before I can stop it.

Why did I lie?

"A shame. A real shame," Glenn shakes his head again. "What with the funeral just days ago, I thought maybe she might've shown up. Or at least called. Just not like that girl. A real shame."

Right, the funeral. Duh.

It takes everything in me not to physically slap my own forehead. Of course, he would be wondering if she had made an appearance or reached out. I can't backtrack now. I just shake my head and tell him the truth. "I really hope I hear from her soon."

I walk into the front door of my childhood home, close it behind me, and slide to the ground leaning against the wall for support. Going through my mom's things feels intrusive. We had no secrets; we all lived in this house for so long together, but it still feels like I am invading her privacy.

After taking a few deep breaths, I pull myself back onto my feet and get to work. I start with the easy stuff like packing up items for donation or boxing up kitchen supplies as though she is only moving to a new house. Mom was always very short and petite – I imagine Abby and I got our height from our dad, as we're both a few inches taller than her – so I know none of her clothes will fit us. I toss those into the donation bag.

As the day goes on, I find less and less to put in the donation bag, and I know I have to start going through some of her other things: books, pictures, legal documents, personal letters. I was planning to leave all of that for tomorrow and call it a day, but I happen upon a box of photos as I push everything to the side. A little nostalgia might be good for me, so I decide to call it a day after I look through this box.

The photos certainly bring back memories, though they were mostly memories of stories Mom would tell us. This box is filled with older pictures, almost all taken before we moved here. Some are of Mom when she was my age or younger, laughing with friends I have never met. Some are from when Abby and I were younger. Abby couldn't have been more than one in some of these pictures. Then I see a photo I don't think I have ever seen before – a picture of the four of us – Mom, Dad, Abby, and me. I've only seen a few pictures of my dad. Mom didn't keep many because it was too painful for her to look at them. I have never seen a family picture with all four of us though. I stick that one in my purse. Abby will want to see it the next time we're together.

Our dad died when we were young. It is one of the reasons we moved to this house. Mom couldn't bear to live in a house with so many memories of him reminding her of what she lost. He was killed in a car accident when I was four. Abby was a little more than one at the time. Mom never talked about the accident, or him, much at all, but we saw how that pain affected her.

We never experienced any real grief over his death, because we never really knew him. We were too young when it happened. I don't know if that made it better or worse for Mom. No one to share in her grief, but also no one to share in her memories.

By the time I finish packing up boxes for the day, it is late afternoon. I check my phone for what feels like the twentieth time, but there are still no texts or calls. Abby never showed up at the house, and she still hasn't reached out. Now I am really starting to worry, so I decide to stop by her place as soon as I finish here.

I begin loading my car with things to drop off at the donation center near my house. When my car can't take any more boxes, I look around for Glenn to say goodbye but don't see him outside anymore. I set aside two of Mom's houseplants for him and leave them on his front step before driving to Abby's apartment.

Her apartment is only a few minutes away from our mom's house, so it's not long before I pull up and find her car parked out front. A wave of anger surges through me, and I try to calm myself down before approaching her door. I seem to need to do that a lot these days.

Abby's apartment is on the ground floor, unlike mine, so as I get closer, I can see that there aren't any lights on inside. *Weird.* It's still light outside, but it seems strange nonetheless.

I knock, but there is no answer. I knock again, louder this time. Still no answer. I try the door handle, but it's locked. I don't know why I would expect it to be unlocked, but I'm disappointed nonetheless.

I'm almost positive I have a spare key to Abby's apartment in my purse. I left everything besides my car keys on the front seat, so I start back towards my car, grumbling to myself the whole way. Picking up my purse, I start digging around for the key as I walk back to the front door. I almost reach the sidewalk, hand still in my purse when something hits me out of nowhere.

No – someone.

In a split second, I realize there is a person now sprinting away from me and towards a running car. He or she – I can't tell underneath the hood of the black sweatshirt they have on – clutches my purse to their chest.

My purse. My phone. My wallet. My car keys that I just tossed back in.

And, of course, Abby's spare key.

CHAPTER 4 – JUNE 2024

RACHEL

I freeze for a few seconds too long. As I begin chasing the hooded person currently in possession of everything I own, – no, I'm not being dramatic – I watch my attacker hop into the passenger seat of a grey minivan and watch that van drive away. I am too far to make out any details. Was it a man or a woman? Was the license plate Florida or another state? What were the letters and numbers on the plate? I couldn't even take any pictures, because they have my phone. Not that I would've even been able to get my phone out in time.

I run back to Abby's front door and begin banging. "Abby, this isn't funny anymore!" I shout. "Open up! We need to talk!"

A neighbor pokes her head out from the apartment directly across from Abby's. The little old woman couldn't have been any younger than seventy, and she is displaying her age perfectly in a ratty, light blue nightgown that looks more like an oversized sweatshirt, flowing all the way to her ankles. I turn to find her grumbling, "Keep it down out here, would you?"

"I'm sorry. It's …" I stumble over my words. "It's my sister. I'm looking for my sister, Abigail Stephens. It's urgent and I'm worried. Do you know her? Have you seen her?"

"Calm down, child," she peers at me over thick lenses, sizing me up. "Abby? No, she hasn't been here in days. I did see her leave with some friends that day she returned from her long trip. Yes, that girl is always leaving, isn't she?" The old woman begins mumbling something to herself that I can't make out as she turns back into her apartment. Then I hear, "Good luck. Keep quiet please. My cats are sleeping."

I roll my eyes as I turn back to Abby's door. So, Abby hasn't been here since the day we argued? That doesn't make any sense.

I walk around the side of the apartment building, hoping to see something, anything, through a window. I get to what I know is the kitchen window and peer through. All the lights are off, there is nothing in her sink or on her table, and her suitcase is sitting in the hallway by the open doorway to the kitchen. It looks as though she came home, set it down, and rushed right over to my place.

Did she even make it back to her apartment after we fought? Or had Ms. Nosy Neighbor seen her sometime that morning? And what friends could she have been talking about? The only friend Abby had in her adult life besides me was Kara, and I was with her the whole night. Could she have met friends on her months-long road trip and brought them back here?

I walk back to Abby's front door. Unsure of what else to do, I knock on the door behind me, and the glare I receive as the door opens is nothing short of terrifying.

"I thought I told you to keep quiet."

"I'm sorry, Ms...?" I pause, waiting for her to give me a name to call her.

The old woman sighs and begrudgingly offers, "McNulty."

"Ms. McNulty, I am so sorry to bother you at this hour." What hour was it anyway? I didn't dare ask. The sun was still out, so not late enough for her to be this grumpy about someone knocking on her door, but I need to let that go for now. "I haven't seen my sister in two days, and she's not answering any calls or texts. I'm starting to worry. Can you please tell me exactly when you last saw her?"

She purses her lips, but answers. "Like I said, the day she came home from her little trip."

"Yes, but morning or afternoon?"

She sighs heavily, clearly irritated. "It was in the morning. Late morning, I think. She left with some people. I didn't recognize them. That's all I know."

So, she did come back after our argument. Yet, the inside of her house doesn't look touched.

"You said she had friends over?"

"Yes, keep up," she snaps. "I won't stand to spend my night repeating myself, child."

"Well, did they go inside at all?" I'm starting to get annoyed with her unreasonable tone but try to keep my cool. *Just get as much information as possible,* I keep telling myself.

"No, no. They never went inside. They stood in the parking lot, talking for a while. She left with them in some van."

I freeze. "Could it have been a grey van?"

"I don't know. I think so, yes. I don't remember. Do you want to hear what I have to say or not?"

I feel the color draining from my face, but I quickly brush the van off as just a coincidence and listen to the rest of what she has to say.

"They were outside. Some young fellows helped her into the back of the van, and I haven't seen her since. But you know, that girl is always in and out." She waves her hand as though brushing off the idea that any part of this conversation might matter. This was all just 'kids being kids' in her mind, and I was upsetting her evening.

"Could you hear anything they were talking about?"

"Of course not, girl. They were in the *parking lot.* You make all this noise for everyone else to hear, but you don't hear very well yourself, do you?"

What is this lady's issue?

"Okay, Ms. McNulty. I'm very sorry to have bothered you."

"That's fine, now. You have a nice evening. And good luck with your sister."

I start to thank her but find the door closing in my face instead. I guess that's all the help I'm getting from her.

I have to figure something out. No one has seen or heard from Abby in two days. Kara would've called way before now if she had heard anything from Abby, but the next chance I get, I can give her a call to be sure. Based on my last attempts, Abby's phone is off. She left with people in a grey minivan – *definitely a coincidence, I tell myself again* – and her apartment still looks untouched.

It may be overkill, but I don't think I have a choice now. I need to walk to the police station. I can't do anything about moving my car right now, but I should probably report my purse, and everything in it, stolen along with seeing if anyone can help me find Abby. The station is only about a mile from where I'm at. Luckily, between growing up near this area and Abby living here now, I know where I'm going without needing a GPS. Once I talk to someone, I can try using their phone to call Kara, too.

At least it's a nice day out, I think to myself, not missing the irony. I suddenly feel bitter about finding myself in this position. Another sick joke, courtesy of the universe. What kind of idiot gets her purse stolen right off her shoulder and doesn't run after the guy? I berate myself for the entire twenty-minute walk.

Once I arrive, I take a few deep breaths before walking into the police station. This is insane. I have never stepped foot inside a police station before, and this place seems way more intimidating than what they look like on TV. Everyone is so focused on what they're doing, and no one here looks approachable. The lighting is dark, and everything I can see is a dull brown or gray color.

I start to walk up to a desk that looks fit for a receptionist when a soft voice from behind me asks, "Can I help you?"

The woman approaching me appears to be in her mid-forties but wears a suit jacket and skirt outfit that looks like it belonged in her grandmother's closet. She smiles at me, friendly enough, as she waits for me to answer.

"Hi, yes. I, uh," I stutter. "I need to talk to someone about filing a missing person's report."

"Okay, dear. Let me get someone for you." Her vocabulary and way of speaking comes from her grandmother too, apparently. Some call it Southern hospitality; I say it ages you a few years.

There are some chairs lined up by the door where I first walked in, so I take a seat there while I wait for the woman to come back. A few minutes later, she comes back and sits in what I had pegged as the reception desk. "Detective Cooper will be right out for you, dear."

"Thank you. Do you mind if I use your phone? Mine was stolen."

"Oh, dear," the woman gasps. "Is that related to the report you want to file?"

"No." I pause, and she gives me a blank look, waiting for me to elaborate. "Well, sort of. Maybe. I'm actually not entirely sure if they're related, but I would like to report both things. I'm sure I can just explain everything when I talk to Detective Hooper." I don't want to have to repeat the whole story of what happened more than once, since I'm still convinced that this is a big overreaction on my part.

"It's, uh, Cooper. Detective Aiden Cooper." I turn to find a man with a hand outstretched, and my jaw drops as I stand to shake it, red slowly coloring my face. I pull myself together in record time, but probably not in time to avoid embarrassing myself.

"Hi, Mr. Cooper. Uh, Detective Cooper. Sorry."

"You can call me Aiden if it'll make all of this easier for you. I'm not big on formality here."

Did I imagine the look the receptionist flashed him?

Aiden, Detective Cooper, whatever. He is gorgeous. He can't be much older than I am. His dark brown spikey hair is cropped short on the sides, and he has the most beautiful hazel eyes I have ever seen. The kind of eyes that are easy to get lost in. The kind of eyes that peer into your soul without your permission.

Somebody coughs.

"Or Detective Cooper is fine."

I blush bright red now. Why am I blushing? Why am I *staring*?

Get your shit together, Rachel.

"No, I'm sorry." I collect myself. "Detective Cooper. My name is Rachel. Rachel Stephens. Something is going on with my sister, and I just want to report her missing so someone can help me find her."

"Okay, Rachel Stephens." He motions to a long hallway lined with offices. I follow him until we get to the end, and we turn left into what I can only assume is his office.

I glance around at the utter lack of personality in the office and feel the need to blurt out, jokingly, "What? No wife or kids?" When he just looks at me, I add, "I'm just kidding. But don't police officers usually have pictures of their families? Kids awards? Finger paintings? That kind of thing?" I'm not even fishing. I just have a terrible case of word vomit that no amount of embarrassment will cure.

"No." There is a slight hint of amusement in his eyes, but not enough to ease my anxiety.

"Is that a no like, '*No, I don't have a wife or kids,*' or a no like, '*No, I don't have those things in here because I don't want the bad guys to know who I care about*'?" I joke. I can't stop the awkwardness from flowing out of me. It's the defense mechanism I manage to keep hidden away until worst-case-scenarios require the service.

He smirks at me like he knows exactly why I am being awkward, as if it's written on my face. "The bad guys don't come into my office. Tell me why you're here, Ms... Stephens, was it?"

Right. I nod. "I need to report my sister missing."

"When was the last time you saw or talked to her?"

"Technically, two days ago."

"Technically?"

"Well, I only saw her for maybe an hour, and we weren't really getting along, so..."

"You argued?" he interrupts. The question doesn't sound suspicious, but I still don't like the way he asked it.

I let out a breath, immediately getting defensive. "Sort of. No, not like a real big argument. I hadn't seen her in months, and she showed up out of nowhere on my birthday of all days, the morning after our mom's funeral and..."

"Wait," he interrupts again, waving a hand now. His brows furrow in confusion as he continues. "So, you hadn't seen her in months? And now it's been two days, and you're reporting her missing? Did something else happen?"

"Yes, can I please just explain? Maybe can I start from the beginning?" My frustration isn't his fault, so I take a deep breath and try to get a hold of my emotions.

He motions with his hand for me to go on, exercising a level of patience that I don't deserve just yet.

I tell the Detective everything from our mom's diagnosis to Abby disappearing from the hospital. From our mom's funeral, and Abby not showing up, to her then showing up at my door and our argument. I told him about the last two days, all the contact I tried to make, and the conversation I had with her neighbor.

"So, you see? I was upset, but who wouldn't be? I just needed time. I tried calling her the very next day, and nothing. Then I went over today, and it looks as though she hasn't even been there except that her unpacked suitcase is sitting by the kitchen. Her car is there, but she's not. And then her neighbor hasn't seen her since Sunday either. And then I got robbed, and…"

"Wait. Wait. You got robbed?" He exclaims, his eyes widening.

"Yeah, I guess I'm here to report that too, but I just wanted to tell you about my sister first. It was outside my sister's apartment. I went to get my purse because her apartment key is in it, and when I was walking back to the front door, someone in a black hoodie just grabbed it and ran. Took off in some grey minivan."

"Grey minivan? Like your neighbor's story?"

"Yeah, I thought that was a strange coincidence, too. But it's just a coincidence, right?"

"Probably. Without knowing the make, model, plate information, and so on, it's hard to know. But every detail matters." He pauses. "Okay, here's what we're going to do. I'm going to file two reports – one for your missing sister and one for the robbery. I need as much detail as possible. Start with your sister. What did she look like?"

"I can bring a picture in as soon as I can get back into my apartment. She has dark brown wavy hair. It used to be long, but the other day she had it cut up to her shoulders. She has these bright, icy blue eyes. My height, around 5' 6". My size, maybe 130 pounds. She's 22, three years younger than me."

"Does she have any scars? Glasses? Tattoos? Any other defining characteristics? And do you know what she was wearing last?"

"She has a scar down her left arm, from around the elbow to about halfway down to her wrist. She's had it since we were kids. She had a tattoo around it when I saw her, though. I think she called it a Phoenix. That was new. And when I saw her, she was just in jeans and a black concert T-shirt. I didn't notice her shoes, but she usually only wears black sneakers."

"Do you remember what band was on her T-shirt? Every detail matters," he repeats.

"I think the band was called Blue October or something. There was a big, grey rose on the front of it."

"Alright, now tell me every detail you can about the person who robbed you, the van, and exactly where you were when this happened."

I tell him every detail I can, but it's not much. I didn't see their face and couldn't even tell if they were male or female. He or she might have been around my height, but it's tough to tell with them running away. I didn't see any license plate details. I tell him everything I had in my purse and that my car would be at my sister's apartment until I could get my spare key.

With that, Detective Cooper walks me back out to the front. "As soon as you get a new phone, call me." He hands me a card with his name and number on it. "That way I know how to reach you if we find anything."

"Thank you."

"Talk to Patty about using our phone to call for a ride. We can also take you home if needed."

"Thanks, but I have to get my spare apartment key from my friend anyway. Thank you for your help, Detective Cooper."

"Seriously, you can call me Aiden. I never did like the titles."

"Thank you, Aiden," I say, only feeling slightly uncomfortable with the first-name basis we are now on.

"Oh, and Rachel?"

"Yes?"

"I'm sorry about your mom. And your sister."

I nod, unable to find any other words, and watch him walk back the way we just came from. I find Patty sitting at the reception desk playing a game of solitaire on her phone. Even her name ages her. Or my judgement could be off and she could just look incredible for her age.

"Hi, Patty. Aid- um, Detective Cooper said I could borrow a phone to call my friend for a ride?" The informality of calling him by his first name makes me feel uneasy the moment I try using it around other people. I'll stick to Detective Cooper for now.

She hands me a phone that looks straight out of the 90s, plugged in behind the desk, phone attached by a spiral cord to the receiver. I have to reach over the countertop to dial Kara's number, and I thank everything in this universe that she has had the same number since we were old enough to have phones.

"Hello?" I hear her skeptical voice.

"Hey, Kara. It's Rachel!"

"Rach! Hi! Have you heard from Abby yet? Whose phone are you calling me on?" She begins rapid-firing questions.

"It's a long story. Look, I need a favor, and no questions until I say so, okay?" I continue without her response. "I need you to pick me up at the Manatee County Police Station as soon as possible."

"Wh-"

"Nope, no questions. I'll explain everything, I promise. But I need a ride first. We can go back to your place and order pizza, and I'll spill everything."

"I'll be there in fifteen minutes!"

She hangs up, and all I can do is sit back down in the chair by the front doors and wait.

A little less than twenty minutes later, Kara walks through the front doors of Manatee County Police Station with a grin that screams mischief. She makes her way over to where I am sitting while I collect what little I have.

"How many times do I have to get this call before you stop getting yourself into trouble? I can't keep blowing your college fund on bail!"

"Kara!" I scold in a whispered hush, cheeks flushing. "You can't joke about that stuff here!" I slap her in the arm as I try to avoid all of the eyes now on us, including Patty, who is trying to hide her laugh behind a stack of folders.

Leave it to Kara to find any opportunity to embarrass me for no reason.

"Okay, okay. Sorry!" Still laughing, she asks, "Now, what's going on?"

I hold a hand up. "Not yet. Car ride home." I am not about to get into everything again with Patty looking over my shoulder. While she was helpful, she also intimidates me, and I don't want her judgement any more than I probably already have it.

"Okay!" Kara holds her hands up in mock surrender. "Where are your things?"

"It's all part of the story. Can we go?"

We head out the door, and I look back to see Detective Cooper – I wasn't really going to start calling him Aiden – standing next to Patty, watching me with an intensity that causes little goosebumps to appear down my arm. I turn and walk faster toward Kara's car, not caring how suspicious it makes me look.

Once I've explained everything, Kara's first question is not what I expect. "So, you're telling me you *walked* all the way to the police station?" She asks the question as though it's the most shocking part of everything I told her.

"Yes. It really wasn't that far, and some of us active people can handle a mile-long walk," I jab. Kara's mocking laugh fills the car and makes the air a little lighter for that moment. She hasn't kept up with running as much as I did after we stopped track. She thrived in the competition way more than I did. Now, I never let her forget I could easily beat her in any race, something I could never do when we were kids.

"You know, I used to outrun you in every race," she echoes my thoughts defensively.

"Yeah. 'Used to' being the operative words." I laugh and she rolls her eyes.

"Why didn't you just call me?" Kara jumps back to her line of questioning, seemingly offended that her phone didn't ring the second I was in any trouble.

"Phone was in stolen purse," I remind her gently.

"Oh right!"

"That reminds me, do you still have the spare key for my apartment?"

"Of course!" she exclaims.

"Would I be able to stay at your place tonight? I need to process all of this, preferably not alone, and then tomorrow I can get into my apartment. I have a spare car key for my car there."

"Of course! Two sleepovers in one week! What are we, thirteen again?"

I try not to think about the reasons I have needed to spend the night at Kara's this week, because I know she is just trying to lighten the mood. "One last thing. Can we stop at one of those convenience stores on the way back to your place? I need some kind of temporary phone." I glance over at her, smirking. "And please don't say 'of course!' again."

"Absolutely!" As she says it, she breaks into a fit of laughter so loud I start to wonder if she is capable of driving. Maybe it's the tension of the last few days or the absurdity of where Kara just picked me up, but I effortlessly join in the contagious laughter. For those few minutes, everything feels normal.

Reality hit again a few minutes later when we pulled up to the mini-mart. I shoot Kara an apologetic look before asking, "Would I be able to borrow some money? No wallet."

She hands me her credit card with a grin. "Go crazy!"

I walk inside myself, promising to be quick. I grab one of those prepaid phones, the biggest bag of Twizzlers they have, some chips, and a couple of cherry sodas. That has always been our sleepover snack spread, and I am craving familiarity tonight.

Kara watches me walk back towards the car and catches the extra bag I'm carrying. "Did you get the good stuff?" I hear before I can even climb into my seat.

"Of course!" I stick my tongue out at her, instantly feeling like a child again. "I got all of our favorites!"

I activate the new phone while we drive the rest of the way to Kara's apartment. As soon as it's active, I pull out the business card Detective Cooper handed me and dial the number at the bottom. It goes right to voicemail. I mouth the word voicemail to Kara right before I hear the tone.

"Hi, um... It's Rachel. Rachel Stephens. I'm just calling to let you know I got a new phone so that you have the number... So that you can call if you find anything. Um.. thank you again for your help. Okay, that's all. So, I'm going to go now. Okay, bye."

As soon as I hang up, Kara bursts into another uncontrollable fit of laughter. I have to remind her that she is still driving while I give her a look letting her know I don't understand what she finds so funny.

"You think the detective is attractive!" Kara explains while catching her breath. There is no question in her response. "Of all the freaking people..."

"What? No, no way. No, I did not." I immediately get defensive and my cheeks start to warm which doesn't help my case.

"Give me a break! You never stutter! Unless you're nervous to talk to a cute boy. Or *man,* since we're adults now and that's a habit you should've left in middle school!" She winks. "You act like I haven't aided you through all your little crushes. Big ones, too. I know when you stutter and why."

"I do not stutter!" I start to argue, but I definitely don't have a case here. "Okay, maybe he's attractive. But there's no way in hell I have a 'crush' on the Detective who is now in charge of helping me find my sister, by the way. In case you forgot that detail already. That would be so wrong on so many levels."

She makes a face, letting me know she isn't buying a word I'm saying, and adds "No one said anything about you *currently* having a crush on anyone."

I resist the urge to smack her as we fall back into more normal conversations. No amount of defending myself will convince her that she's wrong.

When we get back to Kara's place, we both change into sweatpants and settle into the couch for the night. Surrounded by all of our snacks, and with a movie on in the background, I try to figure out what to do next.

"I think I may try to get into Abby's house tomorrow when I get my car, see if I can get in some other way. Maybe the reason she was gone for so long has something to do with where she is now. There might be something in her apartment that will tell me where she was or why she left in the first place."

"You think she ran away again?"

"I don't." I shake my head, sounding more confident than I felt. And then, "I don't know, but I don't think so."

"It is odd that she tried to make everything right with you and then just disappeared again before she had the chance."

"Exactly. And as awful as I was to her the other day, she needed me. She needed to talk to me. That didn't just change overnight." A tear splashes onto my hand and I realize I'm crying. "I wish I had just listened to her, talked to her. Maybe she wouldn't have disappeared again."

"No, Rachel. This isn't your fault. You reacted how any normal person would have. You were hurt, and you had every right to be. You still have the right to feel hurt by what she did. This just happens to be overshadowing that right now, that's all. They'll find her. And then you can talk everything out. You're still sisters. It doesn't matter what happens, you guys always come back to each other. Trust me, I've been a witness to that more than a few times."

I nod my head without any real conviction. "I wish my Mom was here."

"I know. I know." Kara pulls me into a hug, trying to comfort me. "I do, too."

"I'm losing everyone. All at once." More tears begin to fall now.

"Well, you're not losing me, so don't even try."

After a minute, Kara remarks, "We're adults, you know? We really ought to think about adding vodka to our cherry sodas from now on."

I can't control the laugh that follows. It is so out of place for the conversation but so necessary for me in that moment. We laugh until our sides hurt, finally calming down after a few minutes. Turning back to the movie that was already half over, we settle back and watch until we fall asleep.

We both wake up on the couch the next morning, stiff and uncomfortable.

"We are way too old to fall asleep on the couch." I groan.

"Absolutely, we are. I know what will make it better though."

We both say "coffee" in unison.

Kara walks into the kitchen and starts making a pot while I get changed back into my clothes from the day before. I really hope I'm not going to start making a habit out of this.

"You really shouldn't wear the same clothes this many days in a row. If you start to smell too bad, I'll have to leave you outside! People might start to think you're homeless, and then I wouldn't really be able to associate with you anymore. You'd bring my whole vibe down."

I roll my eyes. "I'll try not to have any more life emergencies that prevent me from emotionally or physically returning to my apartment."

"The sarcasm is real with you already," she laughs.

"The day has only begun," I retort. "Do you have my coffee ready?"

"Of course! I live to serve you coffee." She hands my cup to me and disappears into her bedroom to get changed.

"When did you want to go?" I shout from the kitchen.

"Whenever you're finished with your coffee! I'm not going anywhere with you before you've had that!"

I laugh again as she emerges from her room. "Thank you."

"For what?"

"For making me feel somewhat normal the past few days."

"I do believe that's my sole purpose as your forever best friend. I was serious last night. You know I'm not going anywhere. Whatever you need, I'm here for you."

"I know. Thank you."

Once we have both downed our coffees, we drive over to my house. I run in, change into a clean pair of jeans and a T-shirt, and try to clean up quickly. As I walk to the kitchen to find my spare car key, the phone I activated yesterday buzzes. I thought it had to be from Detective Cooper – he was the only one besides Kara who even knew about the phone – but when I see the message, I feel my heart stop for a second, and I know I'm not breathing.

YOU'RE PLAYING A DANGEROUS GAME. YOU'LL LOSE MORE THAN YOUR PURSE IF YOU DON'T STOP LOOKING...

I feel my stomach drop. Stop looking? For Abby? The number is blocked, so I can't see who the text is from. I call Detective Cooper immediately. No answer again. I'm not leaving another voicemail after Kara's stutter analysis yesterday. I will get my car from Abby's apartment and go back down to the police station.

I grab my keys and run out to the car, Kara eyeing me the whole way.

"Hey, what's wrong? You look like you've seen a ghost."

I tell her about the text message.

"You have to call – "

"I already did. Voicemail again."

"Do you want me to drive you to the station?"

"I have to get my car anyway, and Abby's apartment is only a mile from the station. We'll stick to that plan, and I'll drive over from there."

We don't say anything the entire 10 minutes to Abby's apartment. When we finally arrive, I see my car still in the driveway. Part of me is surprised. Whoever stole my purse had my keys. Why would they not take my car? It's not like they don't know where it is.

"Huh, your car is actually still here. There is good in the universe," Kara echoes my thoughts. Sometimes I question whether or not we share one mind.

"I was just thinking the same thing."

"Do you want me to go with you, either inside or to the station?"

"Thank you, but I think this is just something I have to do myself. I promise I'll call you as soon as I know anything."

"If you need anything at all, you call me right away, okay?"

"Okay." I hug her across the center console and climb out of the car.

As soon as Kara pulls out of the driveway, I make my way towards Abby's front door. I will go down to the station as soon as I'm done here. I check everywhere I can think of for a hidden spare key, but I'm not even sure she keeps one anywhere. I'm about to walk around the side of the apartment when my phone rings.

Without checking the number, I answer. "Hello?"

"Rachel?"

"Detective Cooper?" *Finally*, I think to myself.

"Yes. You sound surprised."

"Well, I have been calling you. Did you find anything on my sister?"

"Rachel..." he pauses, and I can feel the pit in my stomach growing. I can feel my anxiety building. I can't handle any more bad news. I need her to be okay, no matter how upset I am with her. I need her to be okay.

"Rachel, the person you reported missing, Abigail Stephens," he pauses longer than he should need to. "Abigail Stephens has been dead since 2003."

CHAPTER 5 – APRIL 2003

SCOTT

I have been working an unreasonable number of hours lately. My job has always been demanding, but the past few months have been unbearable.

It's been just over a year since my little Abby was born. I missed her birthday this year, which I don't think Evelyn will ever forgive me for. I have made every excuse in the book, but none of it matters. I haven't been there for Evey like I promised.

She struggles so much, and I don't know what to do to help. She was supposed to go back to work at the end of last summer, but she never pushed for it. I never pushed her. While it might have lightened my workload, she didn't seem ready. I just kept taking on more clients at work to make sure my girls had everything they needed. At least that's how it started.

Now they have everything they need except for me. When I'm working, I feel like I'm providing; at home, I only feel helpless. I suppose that makes me a coward. I just don't know that I have the strength to pull Evelyn back to who she used to be. I'm not even sure I know how.

Evelyn is more used to the girls' needs anyway, and they're more used to her. Even if I make it home in time for dinner, bath, or bedtime, they just want her to do everything. Rachel will throw a tantrum until Evelyn gets overwhelmed by the crying and gives in to her. She needs to stay awake to feed Abby anyway, so it's easier for her to just do everything. I don't see how that can be true, but that's what she tells me.

I can see the toll all of this is taking on her body and mind, though she never asks for a thing. I know she loves being a mother, and she loves our girls, but something about her is different since Abby was born. I'm not sure she sees it herself.

I feel like more of a failure at home, of course. If I can't help Evelyn, I can't help with the girls, and my hours prevent me from getting to know the girls anyway, then what's the point of going home really? It's a vicious cycle in my head, feeling like I need to be there and then feeling like I don't belong.

I stop at the flower shop across from my office like I do every Thursday since the day we brought Rachel home from the hospital. The sign says they're closed now, but the owner leaves my order on the side of the building when I'm working late. I see the handwritten note he left, letting me know which side of the building the bouquet is on. He started leaving the notes in little codes after I called him after hours, more than once because the flowers had been stolen or ruined by a stray cat. Now he can hide them from thieves and wildlife, and I never have any issues with my Thursday flower pick-up.

As is my new habit, I also stop at the local pub across the street and have a few drinks before I head home. Sometimes I can say that I had to meet a client or that it was a coworker's birthday. Sometimes I don't make any excuses. I know she can smell the bourbon on my breath every time, but she never says anything, and so neither do I. I just grin and bear it when her eyes let me know how much of a disappointment I've become.

Maybe it is a cycle I'll never break out of. The drinking is what leads to her disappointment, but it is also the only thing to numb the hurt of her looking at me that way.

She knows deep down that I'm avoiding coming home, but it's not something she would ever accuse me of. She has too much faith in me to truly have the courage of those convictions. Faith that I will come around, that I will let her in, that this is about more than what she can understand right now. All those excuses only lead to me trying to drown what is remaining of my self-worth.

We used to be so in love. Everything was so easy for us. We laughed together, told each other everything, supported each other through everything. I can't even blame it on having children, because we were still that way after we had Rachel. The changes began toward the end of Evelyn's pregnancy with Abigail. She started to doubt, to pull away more, and I find myself unable to support her through her mental state. I just don't know how.

Can we do this? We already were doing it with Rachel. *Can we afford this?* I work at one of the best law firms in Miami. She doesn't even have to work, and we can afford this. *Am I going to be a good mother to two girls?* She has asked me this question so many times, and I am always baffled by her doubts. She is an amazing mother. She was born to raise girls. And still, this doubt creeps in. Not to mention the mood changes that I assumed were just part of being pregnant, though they were more extreme this time.

I noticed everything. I don't think she knows that I noticed, but I did. I just never threw her the life preserver she needed because I assumed she would figure it out, that it was just a little bump in the road, that she would be okay.

Honestly, I just didn't know how to support her. Instead of facing my shortcomings, I made excuses and chose to avoid her. It felt simpler to deceive myself about my part in letting things deteriorate than confront her directly.

Like I said – a coward.

After a while, I paid my tab at the pub and left a nice tip for my usual bartender. Flowers in hand, I walk down the street back to my office building, get in my car, and drive home.

When I stumble through the doors, a sense of unease grips me. I'm not usually one to rely on intuition — being in my line of work demands a level head — but the atmosphere feels *wrong,* as if the vitality of the place has been drained. It's early enough that Rachel and Abby should be awake, maybe finishing up bath time.

When I get to the kitchen and living room area, no one is there.

I check Rachel's room first, and she is asleep already. I must have just missed her. I close her door quietly, doing my best not to wake her, and walk down the hall. If she is asleep, then maybe Abby and Evelyn have fallen asleep in the rocking chair in Abby's room. I came home more than a few times to the chair still rocking and Evelyn cradling the baby in her arms.

The first time that happened with Rachel, I left them there. I thought the moment was sweet and didn't want to disturb either of them. Of course, Evelyn yelled at me when I awoke the next morning because I didn't consider how dangerous that could be for Rachel if she had been dropped by Evelyn in her sleep. I never made that mistake again with Rachel or Abby.

I open the door, expecting to have to coax Evelyn awake gently, but they weren't in Abby's room either. I check the bathroom in the hall next and then move to our bedroom which I also found empty. As soon as I open the door to the master bathroom, I still, dropping the flowers I didn't realize I was still carrying.

I find my wife clutching our baby girl, cowering on the bathroom floor, rocking back and forth. I can't see her face, but I know she is sobbing by the quick rise and fall of her shoulders.

I can't see Abigail's face either, and at some point, it occurs to me to wonder whether she can even breathe being held so tight to Evelyn's chest.

My mind doesn't fully comprehend what is going on until Evelyn finally dares to look up at me, peering from beneath her eyelashes still as though afraid to show her entire face. All life has gone from her normally glowing gaze. Tears are falling, but she doesn't look sad. She looks lost, dead, like there is a massive hole newly formed inside of her that I can never even begin to repair.

"It. Was. An accident." Barely a whisper. I'm not even sure I heard her correctly at first.

As soon as I start to process that something here is very, very wrong, I jump into action trying to figure out what Evelyn needs. I will get help. I will do whatever I need to in order to make this better because this can be fixed. Whatever happened here was only an accident, and Evelyn sitting on the floor in tears, blaming herself isn't going to make things any better.

She keeps repeating only those four words, barely audible. "It was an accident." Still rocking, there was no life left in her voice either.

"It's fine. We can fix this. I can fix this," I repeat, as though saying those words will make them true.

I can fix this.

I can fix us.

I will fix us.

I walk over to where Evelyn sits by the bathtub, and gently reach for Abigail, wondering if I should set her in her crib or take her with me. "I will fix this, Evelyn. I promise."

She's sleeping. Abigail is sleeping. I will go find help for Evelyn.

I know this is the night I go mad, too, because I leave Evelyn, alone and shaking, on the bathroom floor without even the comfort of a hug to hold her together. I step on the flowers I dropped to the floor as I take my little girl to lay her down in her crib. I leave to get help without another word.

I don't come back for two days.

CHAPTER 6 – JUNE 2024

RACHEL

I don't know how long I stop breathing. One second? One minute? An hour could have gone by, and I wouldn't have noticed.

I heard a voice on the other end of the phone that was somehow still being held to my ear, clutched so tight I could feel my knuckles whiten. Detective Cooper. Right. Suddenly, I am forced back into the present moment, breathing resumed, heart restarted.

"I'm... I'm sorry. You're wrong," I tell him, shaking my head vigorously. The words come out more calmly than I feel.

"Rachel, I'm telling you that according to our database..."

"I JUST SAW HER THREE DAYS AGO!" All the calm I felt 5 seconds ago is replaced by a sudden hysteria. Just like that, I lose all control of my emotions, my volume, and my hands as they start to shake. What Detective Cooper is saying just cannot be true. I need to stay calm and tell him, rationally, that there is just no way.

"Rachel, listen..."

"No, you listen. Please." I interrupt, my voice taking on a softer assertiveness. "There's been a mistake. I've had a sister my whole life. You need to check again. Your database is wrong. Please, just check again."

"Rachel." His tone changes from comforting to stern. He clearly has something to say and is done with my outbursts and denials. "You don't have a picture."

"My phone was stolen!" I argue.

"Which brings me to my other point. You had a key to an apartment that was also miraculously stolen right before reporting this supposed sister missing. Along with the phone that has all your pictures on it. I'm not saying I don't believe you. But now we find your sister in our system with a record of death from April of 2003. Are you hearing me? That means she's been dead for more than 20 years. All of this comes just days after you lose your mom. I know you're under a lot of stress, and grieving, but you understand how this looks, right?"

I'm crying now. I check my surroundings making sure Ms. Nosy Neighbor hasn't come outside to see what all the screaming is about, making sure no one can see me in the state I'm in right now.

"Detective Cooper. Aiden. Whatever you want me to call you. My sister is missing, and I need to find her." I'm calm again, but there is an iciness to my tone that frightens me. "She is the only thing in this world that I have left. She's *not* dead. She's *not* a figment of my grieving imagination. You *are* wrong, and if you won't help me, I will find her myself."

I hang up the phone and sit down in the grass with my back up against the side of the building. My emotions are overwhelming me, and I need to breathe. I pull my knees toward my chest and rest my head on top of them while I take a few deep breaths.

Dead since 2003? That doesn't even make sense. I grew up with her. I've known her all my life. We played Barbies as kids and did each other's hair through middle and high school. Abby, Mom, and I had each other's backs because we were all we had. There is no way none of that was real. Mom grieved for months, believing she wouldn't see her daughter again before she passed away.

Although part of my mind starts to wander, to wonder if there were any other times Abby went "missing" from my memories that I simply don't remember.

I shake my head at myself. Before I can convince myself that I am going crazy, I remember that Kara knows Abby, too. She grew up with her along with me. Even though I no longer have her key, I am standing outside of Abby's apartment. Her neighbor knows her. She isn't overly fond of my sister, or anyone it seems, but she knows her. She's very clearly alive – I wasn't going to let my mind wonder about the past few days – and something is very clearly wrong here.

My mind switches gears to some arguably more important questions. Someone had to have changed that record. Why would information about Abby's life, or death, change? Who would have access to it? When was it changed, and who would need to change it?

I can ask Detective Cooper after I've calmed down a bit more. And after I've apologized to him for my outburst and for not hearing him out. He may have access to that kind of information.

Something isn't adding up. The more I hear, the more that doesn't make sense, and the more I worry about Abby and where she could possibly be. If Detective Cooper is truly willing to help me, maybe he can help me connect some of these dots.

After a few minutes, my breathing starts returning to normal, and my mind clears. Now, it is even more important for me to get into her apartment. There is no way I can get in through the front door, but thankfully she is in a 1st floor apartment.

I walk around the back to check the windows, but nothing is open.

Why would anything be open?

A quick glance around tells me that no other neighbors face her back window. The back of her building looks out over a wide-open field, completely flat and covered by tall grass and weeds. I guess no one does any lawn maintenance back there. There is at least a mile or two until the next group of buildings. It's Wednesday afternoon, so the chances of other neighbors hearing what I'm about to do is slim. Most people should be working – I just hope most people work out of the comfort of an office and not the comfort of their own living room.

I make a mental note to apologize to Abby when I find her, pick up a brick from the pile I passed on the side of the building, and throw it through her window. I'll fix it, too.

I reach inside through the hole I made, unlock the window, and push it open so that I can climb through. Once inside, I scan my surroundings. Everything is so neat. Way neater than I would expect for any place my sister has occupied. She was always a little neater than I was, but her space certainly felt lived in when I had visited here on other occasions. Now, it looks almost staged for a showing. It feels empty, though there is a thick layer of dust on everything. I suppose there would be after four months.

Abby's suitcase is still by the entryway that leads into the kitchen – right where I saw it the other day.

So, she hasn't been back here. I don't know why I was expecting anything different, but I could feel my stomach sinking and my heart racing regardless. The more I look around, the more I hear alarm bells going off in my head.

It is definitely *too* neat. No dishes in the sink, trash empty except for a few pieces of mail. I check the dates on the bills I find, and they are from February, before Abby had actually run off. Nothing is on the counter or the table. I check the fridge. Empty. I make my way through the living room and into the bedroom. No empty water bottles lying around, no half-read book on her nightstand, and no clothes in the hamper. I check one of her dresser drawers because I'm starting to feel like maybe I am crazy. Maybe no one even lives here, or maybe I just broke into a random stranger's house.

I breathe an unreasonably loud sigh of relief when I find the drawer full of all Abby's clothing. The rest of the drawers are full, too. Relief floods over me as I clutch a handful of her t-shirts to my chest. Someone – no, Abby – does live here. The relief doesn't last long as I realize *all* of her clothes are still here. Why would she go anywhere without clothes? Without her jeans or favorite sweatshirt?

I continue to look around and notice that all of her pictures are gone, too. All the pictures of us, of our mom, of any friends, gone. Anything truly personal is gone. There is nothing to say that this is Abby's apartment as opposed to anyone else's. Nothing except her clothes which I recognize – *but who else would?* – and the bill from February. It's almost as if she had planned to disappear.

But she came back, I remind myself. She needed me, and, even though I let her down, she wouldn't run away again without talking to me first.

Unless she felt like I would never listen.

Would she really believe that?

Or unless she was giving me a reason why she had to leave again.

She wouldn't do that to me.

I am mentally kicking myself when…

The bill.

It has her name on it. It's a utility bill for this apartment. I run back to the kitchen to grab the piece of mail from where I set it on the counter.

Looking at it again, I confirm that it's her name and address across the top. I fight back tears of relief at the confirmation that Detective Cooper is wrong. I knew that already, of course, but now I have proof. I look through all of the drawers in her kitchen for anything else to prove that she's alive and that she was here.

I make my way back into the living room and look in the drawers in her TV stand, end tables, anything that could hold a piece of her. I don't find anything personal anywhere. Until I remember her suitcase. If she had anything that would say where she went or why, it may be in there.

I open the suitcase to find some clothes that I don't recognize and basic toiletries. I begin to doubt that I'll find anything useful when I notice a zipper along the inside edge. I give that a try and find a gas receipt from a small town outside of Miami.

Why was she in Miami?

I dig around the small space again until I pull out an envelope and a small picture. I turn the picture over to find my mom, Abby and me laughing into the camera. It was taken right after Abby's high school graduation. We were all dressed up to go to a nice celebratory dinner, but none of us could keep a straight face for the camera. I have the same picture hanging on my wall – it was always one of our favorites. I swear I feel my heart stop for a few seconds as I feel a pang of longing for that moment. For all of us to laugh together again.

Then, confusion overcomes me when I see what is written on the envelope.

The front reads "Evelyn, My Darling Wife."

Our dad died in a car accident when I was only 5 years old. Abigail was a little more than 2 at the time. Mom never remarried. She never talked about our dad, and, if she did keep anything of his, she kept it very private. If this was a letter from our dad to our mom, what was Abby doing with it? How did she come across it? Did Mom know she had it? Why didn't she ever tell me about it?

A shadow by the front door makes me jump out of my thoughts and back to the present moment. I would have to save the letter for later. I need to get out of here before I get caught. I fold up the letter and put it in my pocket along with the utility bill I grabbed from Abby's trash can. I wait by the front door for the shadow to leave, and then I head out.

Walking towards the parking lot, I suddenly see a figure step out from the side of the building. Before I can react or realize what's going on, I hear a voice say, "I thought I'd find you here." Detective Cooper walks up beside me, a knowing grin on his face.

I forgot, quite literally overnight, just how handsome he was, and it takes me a few extra seconds to collect myself. I never thought of myself as particularly fond of uniforms, but he wore his well. I snap out of my trance when I remember I need to somehow explain how I just came out of an apartment I don't have a key for.

Under pressure, I blurt out, "I have a key."

Really, Rachel? A blatant lie? He knows you don't have a key! I internally shake my head at myself, scolding my stupidity, but I keep my face stoic.

"The same key that was in the purse you reported stolen yesterday?" His smile reveals dimples I hadn't noticed last night.

My face falls. "I'm not going to answer that."

"Yeah." He is gazing at me with a look I can't figure out, almost like he is amused but still trying to act professionally. Like I'm somehow making that difficult for him, but he doesn't mind.

"What are you doing here, anyway? Spying on me?" I snap, reverting to my earlier annoyance.

"Well, you did mention that Abigail has a neighbor. I came to talk to her."

"Good luck with that," I laugh.

"Why? Is she tough to talk to?"

"A little cranky, I guess. She didn't exactly appreciate me banging on Abby's door before."

"Is that why you went through the window today?"

All the color drains from my face. Suddenly, I find myself playing defense. "Look, I know you won't understand, but this is her apartment. I have proof. This was in her trash can." I hand him the utility bill I found and point out both her name and address on the bill. "I needed to get inside, because I needed to look for anything that could help me find her. I am going to replace the window, and I'm sure she won't mind when she hears why I did it."

"And did you find anything besides the utility bill?"

I hesitate for just a second, but I don't know what the letter means yet. "Here's a picture of the three of us, my family. When I saw Abby the other day, her hair was cut up to her chin, but otherwise she looks the same. The picture is only about 4 years old. It does look like the place has been cleaned out of anything personal, although all her clothes are still here."

Detective Cooper considers this for a minute before responding. "I'm not going to say anything about the window. I understand why you did it."

Shocked by his kindness now, I wonder aloud, "Do you have any siblings?"

"No, just me." He looks away, sad, for a moment before turning back to face me.

"Look Detect-"

"Aiden." He cuts me off.

"Okay, Aiden. I'm sorry I yelled at you earlier."

"I understand. Same reason you broke the window. This is your sister."

"Yes, but it's more than that. She's all I have left. I know something is wrong. She's never done anything like this. At least when she ran off before, she checked in occasionally. She needed me in the coffee shop the other day, and I wasn't there for her. I didn't want to hear her out. If something bad has happened, I don't think I'll ever be able to forgive myself. She's real. She's alive. And she's all I have left." I emphasize the last part again.

"I understand, Rachel. I'm not giving up. That's why I'm here."

I nod, trying to convey with my expression alone how grateful I am.

"How did you get here anyway?"

"Oh, Kara dropped me off. The girl who picked me up last night. She has a spare key to my apartment where I had a spare key to my car. She brought me here to pick my car up."

"Was she involved in your breaking and entering plans?"

"No, I didn't decide to do that until I was here already. After talking to you, actually."

He winces, recalling our earlier conversation, and then replies, "Good, I won't have to arrest her then."

I look at him quickly only to find him laughing. My shocked expression turns into a glare.

"Det – Aiden, thank you for understanding. I'm going to go back inside to cover up the window with a sheet for now, and then I have to head over to my mom's place. I'm still cleaning her house out."

"Would you like any help with the window before you go?"

"That would actually be great, thank you." I almost forgot that I need to cover it up in my rush to leave, and I wasn't thinking about the logistics of actually doing it myself. Help would be nice.

Once back inside the apartment, I find an old sheet while Aiden collects unused nails from the spaces where pictures used to hang. After that, and after sweeping all the glass up, the simple task of nailing the sheet into the window frame only takes a few minutes. While we work, Aiden starts asking me questions that feel personal, but somehow not invasive.

We talk about where I was born, when I moved here. I tell him how and when my dad died and how I believe we only moved here so my mom could have a fresh start. Without seeming like

I'm still pleading my case, I get to tell him all about Abby, what she means to me, how close we were up until a few months ago.

I feel more like I am unloading on a friend than a detective or a stranger, which he still technically is. For whatever reason, though, he seems content to just be present, listen, play the role of shoulder-to-cry-on.

When I finally look over at the clock on the stove, almost an hour has gone by.

I stand up from the kitchen table I don't remember sitting down at and apologize for needing to cut the conversation short.

"I'm so sorry to keep you. I'm sure you have to get back to work."

"It's okay, Rachel," he promises as he starts to stand.

We both make our way out the front door and down the sidewalk, Aiden walking me to my car.

"Hey, Rachel?" he asks before making his way back to the apartments.

"Yes?"

"I'm sorry you're going through all of this." He sounds so genuine, and I can't wrap my head around why he's being so nice to me.

"Yeah." It's all I can say.

"I'll call you if anything new comes up or anything changes," he promises.

"Thanks, Aiden." The smile he flashes when I call him by his first name sends a ridiculous amount of unwanted butterflies through my stomach.

I don't know why, but I have a distinct feeling that I can trust him when he says he will help me. I hope I'm not misjudging him. I hope I'm not wrong.

CHAPTER 7 – JUNE 2024

RACHEL

I drive to my mom's house in complete silence. I keep replaying the conversation I had with Aiden in my head over and over. I'm more than determined to find Abby, with or without anyone's help, but it would be nice to have his.

I did wonder where his change of heart had come from though. One minute, he was making it seem as though he thought I was certifiable. The next, he's dropping by to interview neighbors. I appreciate the change, and the help, but my mind can't get past the *why?*

It occurs to me that 'he's just doing his job' is a perfectly reasonable and logical explanation. I need to stop overthinking everything.

I still have no intentions of relying on anyone but myself, because he is, in fact, doing his job, while I'm trying to find my sister. I still have work to do at the house, a lot of work, so I can collect my thoughts while I continue packing her things.

When I finally pull up to the house, I stare at it for a few moments again. Even though I have been here twice in as many days, it still feels surreal to step into a place where I expect there to be so much life and energy but find myself lonely instead.

I was 5 years old when we moved from a small town outside of Miami to the Tampa area we live in now. It happened just a month after our dad passed away. I always imagined my mom struggling to live in the same house where she had so many cherished memories.

She referred to our new home as our "fresh start," but there was always a glint in her eyes when she said that - a sparkle that as a 5-year-old, I couldn't grasp was actually just tears forming.

I understand, now, stepping into a house filled with ghosts of memories past, memories that might be too painful to live in every day.

For Abby and me, the move was abrupt and chaotic. There were boxes everywhere for months at the new house. We ate on paper plates and slept in sleeping bags for what felt like an eternity. Within a few days, I went from playing in our backyard, decorating the fridge with the artwork I made at summer camp, helping Mom with Abby's bath time, to everything I know being boxed up and waking up in a new house. I suppose any kid would feel that way though.

Abby was only 2, so she had no memory of our life before.

A realization dawns on me that neither of us truly had memories of our life before, of our father. My stomach sinks as I decide that must have made it harder for our mom. Not only did she have to grieve her husband's loss, but she had to do it alone and in a new place.

I feel that way now, still unable to force myself out of my car. Memories flood my mind, and my train of thought brings fresh tears to the surface. I can feel them threatening to spill over as the weight of my emotions becomes overwhelming, compounded by everything I've faced in less than a week. I rest my head on the steering wheel and give myself permission to feel and process it all.

I don't know how long I have been crying when a knock on my window startles me out of my hysterics. I look up, wiping my eyes, to find Glenn standing outside my door.

"Rach, you okay?" he shouts. I wonder if he knows he doesn't need to yell so loud.

All I can do is nod silently in response. With a press of a button, I turn off my car and open the door slowly. Glenn envelops me in a hug that feels awkward, strained, but I understand how concerned he must be after witnessing me sobbing into my steering wheel for God knows how long.

"Sweetie, what's wrong?" I can hear that concern in his voice. *Yep, definitely worried.*

Unfortunately for me, I still feel like I'm mid-panic attack. I can't breathe, I can't speak.

My body is on autopilot as he begins ushering me towards his driveway, towards his front door. "Come on, let's get you some water." Glenn's hands on my shoulders are the only thing guiding me to my destination.

As I settle into a seat at Glenn's kitchen table, clutching a cold glass of water, I glance up to see him staring at me intently. "Do you want to tell me what that was all about?" His voice carries an edge I can't quite place, until I remind myself that he had just witnessed me in the midst of a complete breakdown in my mother's driveway.

Still, I wasn't able to speak yet. Instead, I take a sip of water, trying to compose myself, while Glenn repeats his question with a hint of sternness in his tone.

"I just couldn't hold everything in anymore," I confess, my voice strained and barely audible. "I started crying and... and I just couldn't stop." I shrug my shoulders as if to downplay my emotional outburst, but embarrassment washes over me, prompting me to lower my gaze to the floor. Allowing myself a moment there, I gather my composure.

"Hmph." Glenn responds, his scrutiny intensifying, now tinged with skepticism. "Does this have anything to do with Abigail?"

My head snaps up, startled by his question. Meeting his penetrating gaze, I struggle to hide my surprise.

"What?" I manage to utter, my voice still little more than a whisper.

"Abigail," he repeats calmly. "She didn't come to the funeral, and the other day you said you hadn't heard from her. I just thought you might be worried about her. I'm sure she would've shown if she could though. She wouldn't leave you alone without a reason." He shrugs his shoulders, a picture of nonchalance, while he sips his water, but his tone conveys a different message, hinting that he might know more than he's letting on.

That's crazy though. I brush that thought off as nothing more than stress-induced paranoia and say, "Oh, yeah."

Why am I so on edge about Abby whenever he brings her up? Of course, it's natural for him to ask about her. I've lied to him twice now, but he doesn't know that. Why would he have any reason to believe the situation is worse than her just not coming home? Why is he speaking about her like she's done something wrong? Like he knows why she didn't show up at the funeral?

Despite these thoughts, I'm not ready to confess. I don't want anyone feeling sorry for me any more than they already do. I need to stop reacting so strongly whenever Abby is mentioned, or he might start pressing me.

"I don't want to pry but..." Glenn starts cautiously.

"Good, then don't." I cut in sharply, my tone more cutting than I intended, but I am done talking about all of this for today. "No, I haven't heard from Abby. My mother also died, and I'm alone. Alone. I just want time to wallow in my own pathetic grief over losing my entirely too small family while I clean out the house I grew up in and figure out how I move on with my life without both my sister and my mom."

Glenn is left stunned and silent, which immediately fills me with guilt. Trying to salvage the situation, I quickly add, "I really appreciate your concern, I do. Glenn, you've always been there for us, for Evelyn. I just need a little space to figure everything out. I'm sorry for worrying you today, but I have to go."

I make my way back over to my mom's house, stopping at my car to grab the phone and jacket I left in my state of unraveling and then head inside, doing my best to focus on my breathing. I do not want to start crying again, whether I have witnesses or not.

I'm left more than a little shaken from my encounter with Glenn. He had to have been coming from a place of concern — he's known Abby and me practically our whole lives, and he was best friends with Evelyn. And yet… Something about how stern he sounds leaves me feeling rattled. He never spoke to either of us that way before. For him to see me so broken and still have that edge in his voice is frightening. The way he asked about Abby felt off. His tone, his words, and his body language did not match, which left me feeling uncomfortable. It was the first time in my entire life that I didn't believe his concern was completely genuine, but I have no idea why I feel that way.

Maybe I am starting to get paranoid.

Instead of dwelling on the unsettling encounter with Glenn, I throw myself into the task at hand: completing the packing of Mom's house. Most of her clothes are already boxed up, so I turn my attention to the bedrooms, mostly unchanged since Abby and I moved out. The posters we kept on our walls as kids have come down, but the furniture is still the same.

Starting with my own room, memories flood back as I pack up old clothes and load them into my car. I repeat the process in Abby's room, planning to leave her clothes at her apartment in case she returns. The beds were stripped, dressers emptied, and walls cleared of framed pictures that held some of our best memories.

Abby's closet seems to be a storage area for all of Mom's preserved treasures. I find boxes filled with old books, forgotten knick-knacks, and remnants of hobbies she briefly pursued — a testament to her desire to learn and embrace new things… Crochet needles, dusty easels, and an unused yoga mat bring a wide grin to my face as I hear her old excuses for 'moving onto the next exciting thing' replay in my head. As I continue to filter through her belongings, I realize there is more here than I expected. I pull out a large filing cabinet that promises to be a project for me at a later date and find a medium-sized, burnt orange box behind it.

The box looks old and flimsy; it's covered in dust as though it hasn't been touched since we moved into the house. Maybe even longer ago than that. It looks like years of being moved around, tossed, and left under piles of other things had left dents and marks on every square inch. On closer inspection, I see my dad's name, Scott, written in small capital letters and crossed out on the side.

My curiosity gets the better of me. I pull the box onto the bed and begin going through it. At first glance, there isn't anything having to do with Scott in the box. I take out a very old picture of Abigail and me from just after she was just born. There was another framed picture of all four of us in the backyard of our old house. It's similar to the one I took the other day, but this one has Mom's garden on full display behind us. There are some lightly used baby toys – a teething ring and a little rabbit with a rattle inside.

All of this was sitting on top of what looked to be an old baby blanket.

The blanket is a white and light blue crochet blanket with purple lettering across one of the edges. I open it up all the way to find the name Victoria stitched in cursive lettering across the top.

Victoria?

Did Mom start crocheting early? Did they originally plan on naming their second-born Victoria? Honestly, the blanket looks old enough that they might've planned on naming *me* Victoria. But why label this box, with two pictures, toys, and a baby blanket that doesn't belong to us, Scott? Why even pack up two random baby toys and box them away in the bottom of a closet forever? Nothing about the contents of this box makes any sense.

Or maybe it was just packed up and forgotten when we moved here. Mom threw it in the closet and didn't remember. But this had been Abby's closet, and she never mentioned the box before, so Mom had to have moved it in here at some point.

Another wave of grief hits me as I stare at the burnt orange box. So many questions flood my mind, questions I may never know the answers to. The only person who could've answered them is gone. It feels like every unanswered question adds another brick to the weight of my chest, making it hard to breathe.

I push through the feeling, deciding to deal with the box later. I throw the contents back into the box and leave it on the bed. In desperate need of a break now, I head to the kitchen to grab a water bottle. I down it in a few quick gulps, hoping the cool liquid will somehow clear my head. As soon as I feel my breathing return to normal, I check my phone, but there's still nothing from Abby. No messages from Aiden or anyone else either. The silence feels heavy, like another layer to the grief that I'm already struggling to bear.

For a moment, I just stand there, feeling lost in the quiet house that used to be so full of life. My mind races, trying to grasp onto something—anything—that can give me a sense of direction or purpose. But all I find is more questions and the ever-present absence of the ones I love.

I take a deep breath, trying to steady myself. There's still so much to do and wallowing in my grief won't help anyone. I decide to tackle another part of the house, maybe the living room or the attic. Anything to keep moving, to keep the weight from becoming too much to bear.

I decide not to return to Abby's old room. Instead, I tackle the office, sorting through piles of paperwork and organizing them into boxes near the filing cabinet I found earlier. I pack up the TVs and other electronics from every room and put all of the non-perishable food from the kitchen into a box for donation.

By the end of the night, I've amassed a sizable "Donation" pile and an even larger "Trash" pile. Staring at them, exhaustion overwhelms me. How could my mother's whole life be reduced to these two piles? A wave of nausea sweeps over me, and I head back to the kitchen for another bottle of water.

I check my phone for what feels like the hundredth time as I sit down at the table. My stomach drops when I find another text from a blocked number waiting to be read.

YOU'RE NEXT IF YOU DON'T STOP SNOOPING AROUND IN THINGS THAT DON'T CONCERN YOU.

What does that even mean? What am I snooping around in? I am only trying to find Abby, and I'm not even doing a great job of that. Am I snooping by clearing out my mom's house? I am starting to wonder whether or not I should tell Aiden about the text messages, but decide to sleep on that. It is time to call it a night anyway, so I can think about calling him about this in the morning.

I still can't figure out how the sender would've gotten the number to a phone I just bought off a convenience store rack or what the point is. The texts don't even mention Abby.

Could these cashiers have a way of hacking the phones they sell? Getting the numbers out of their system once the phones are activated? Was this all just a poorly-timed prank?

All questions that Aiden might be able to answer, I suppose. Then again, I remember that Aiden is one of only two people who have this number, and I'm finding myself less certain about who I can trust.

My drive home is uneventful. I consider calling Kara to talk to her about how strange Glenn had acted earlier, but she might accuse me of starting to get a little paranoid, and I do not have any desire to be lectured with logic right now. The texts make me feel like I am decidedly not paranoid, but my mind jumps again to the only two people who have my new phone number. The second I start not trusting Kara is the second I decide that maybe I am losing touch with reality. Still, I don't make the call.

When I finally get home, I only have enough energy to shower and climb into bed. As I'm settling under the covers, though, I see something sticking out of the jeans that are sprawled across the floor.

The letter.

I pick it up off the floor, climb back into bed, and read it until I fall asleep. The shock of what I'm reading keeps me re-reading for as long as I can keep my eyes open and brings with it the nightmares that would keep me tossing and turning for the entire night.

CHAPTER 8 – MARCH 2004

SCOTT

Abigail is two.

I don't miss her birthday this year.

I haven't been able to miss much lately. The guilt won't allow me to. I still work too many hours, but fear keeps me coming home for the important things. Any time I might miss something, my mind takes me back to the night I almost missed something unforgivable.

It feels as though our whole neighborhood is here today, and that always makes me nervous, too. I can't expect Evelyn to be on the lookout or keep a close eye on the girls all by herself, so I need to.

We live at the end of a very long street which makes the front of our house optimal for block parties, gatherings, celebrations of any kind. We don't often participate, but we don't mind the commotion either.

Today, we are the commotion. We have charcoal grills going where the blacktop reaches grass, we set up one of those small moon bounces for the kids, and we ordered all kinds of treats for kids and adults alike.

I walk around, nodding my hellos and smiling at everyone I pass. I don't really know anyone, though. We don't have family nearby, and my hours make friendships impossible to maintain, but I do recognize some faces.

Evelyn doesn't really know anyone here either, not beyond the acquaintance level, but she has fewer excuses than I do.

That's our neighborhood though. Any excuse to gather, even if you don't know the hosts.

I do my best to keep my bitter thoughts from reflecting on my face. I shouldn't care so much about not having friends or about faking my way through block parties. I just feel on edge when I need to be in the role of a protector. That's what these parties do to me.

I should be grateful we even have this moment at all given everything that happened last year.

It's been a year.

And yet, that night will live with me forever.

Evelyn has not looked at me the same as she did before. I think the only person she looks at the same now is Rachel.

With everything I've sacrificed, I'm left with a wife who despises me but who still expects me to be present for children who don't even know me. Children who may never know me if things keep going this way.

I was able to fix everything about that night – everything but us.

I take a sip of the soda I have in my hand and find myself craving something stronger. Walking towards the house, I can feel Evelyn's stare burning a hole in my back. I simply don't care. When I get inside, I dump the soda into the sink and replace the contents of my cup with the McCallan I keep hidden away for special occasions.

This feels like one of those occasions.

"At your daughter's birthday party?" The judgement, cold and unforgiving, comes from behind me.

"Not now, Evelyn. Please." I sigh audibly, feeling defeated already, without turning to face her.

"You're a coward, you know that? You think I'm not still haunted by everything that happened last year? That I don't blame myself for everything? But someone must raise these girls. Not all of us can hide behind our desks or our booze. It would be nice for you to be present today of all days. You complain over and over that they don't know you, but you don't even give them a chance."

"I said not now, Evelyn. Please. Please." My voice breaks on the last word, and I feel myself shrink down. What am I turning into? Since when did my emotions become so strong that they had the power to overwhelm me? No wonder she thinks I'm a coward.

"Then when?" she bites back. "Because it's been almost a year and you're still getting drunk at a two-year-old's birthday party. You might as well be working if you refuse to be present at home."

I turn toward her then, feeling the menacing look take form on my face, and I watch her flinch. "You would love that, wouldn't you? You would never have to look me in the eye and see your faults staring back at you. I am the constant reminder you wish you could get rid of."

"Scott, that's not…"

I cut her off. "This is your fault, Evelyn. This is all your fault. Now you have to let me deal with the consequences however I see fit." There was an ice in my voice that I didn't fully recognize. I hear it on occasion, but it never feels like it's my voice speaking. It's like an out-of-body experience, but I don't like the monster inside me taking over my voice, my thoughts, my words.

I watch as Evelyn stumbles back a step and takes a seat on the couch behind her. I just placed all of my guilt, all of my frustration, squarely on the shoulders of the woman I once loved. Still love, I think. A woman who is struggling right alongside me but handling it better than I ever could.

Yet, I don't have it in me to take the words back.

There was a time I would've done anything for this woman. There was a time when I *did* everything for her, made every sacrifice for her. Now, I can't console her, can't look at her as she starts weeping on the couch. I can't look her in the eye anymore – the very thing I just accused her of.

I couldn't fix me. I couldn't fix her. I couldn't fix us.

We both remain still for a few minutes until Evelyn finally stands, wiping away her tears with a tissue. She walks out the door, out towards the party that was still going on outside. Before reaching the door, she turns to face me, glaring at me with so much venom that I know this will be the moment she never forgives me for. Mine will be the words that finally do us in.

Evenly stands suddenly then, heading for the front door. I see her pause in the doorway before she says to me, "We both made unforgivable mistakes and have now made our bed. I think it's about time we get back to laying in that bed together. Our girls need us. Both of us. That's all there is to it."

I down my drink as soon as the door closes behind her and pour myself another one. As I get back to the party, two questions play on a loop in my head.

How did we get here?

Can we ever get back to who we used to be?

If I can't fix this, I'm not sure I can handle the weight of the fallout.

CHAPTER 9 – JULY 2004

EVELYN

Nights can be the hardest for me, especially the nights Scott works late. That happens to be most nights these days.

He works so hard for us, for me, to be able to support us and allow me to stay home with the girls. I love watching them grow and learn right before my eyes. I never had to miss a first step or a first word. Sometimes, though, I wonder about going back to work. Adult interaction is something that can be easily taken for granted. Mostly I think I am just missing my husband, and I tell myself that if I work more hours, maybe he can work less.

Things have been difficult between us since Abigail was born. Really, things have been difficult for me.

And then I made things difficult for both of us when...

I shake my head, not giving any weight to where my train of thought is headed. I know things have been especially hard on Scott, too. But he still comes home with flowers every Thursday, just like he has since the day we brought Rachel home from the hospital. Being our first child and having some minor difficulties before we could officially bring her home, that day was extra special for us.

Even after we fight, even after I see all sense of fight left his eyes, that is the one thing that doesn't change between us.

In the last year, we had moments where I don't think we recognized each other, but we always came back to each other at the end of the day. Every marriage has that at some point or another, right?

I am standing in the kitchen, cleaning up dinner while Rachel plays with Abby in the living room. I wash the dishes quickly, so I won't have my back to them for long, but take my time cleaning up the rest of the kitchen as I watch for the phone to ring.

While Scott works late often, it isn't like him to not call.

When I can't stall any longer, I collect the girls for bath time and bed. Rachel is a tremendous help with Abby's bath time but always wants to play on her own. I started giving them their baths together so that Rachel could play and help at the same time, which saved me so much work.

I stare down at my little girls, wondering how I got so lucky.

Once the girls were bathed and put to bed, I checked the phone in the kitchen to make sure I haven't missed any calls. There is no light flashing on the phone, so I make my way into my bedroom to get myself ready for bed. It's getting late for Scott to still be working, but he has always been prone to the occasional all-nighter or coming home after I'm already asleep. He usually lets me know, though.

When I walk into the bedroom, I stop dead in my tracks. There is something sticking out of the book sitting on my bedside table. It was the corner of something – a small note or an envelope of sorts – that I hadn't seen there this morning.

Everything in my body screams that something is wrong. There is a pit forming in my stomach, but I have no evidence to support the anxiety suddenly washing over me.

I pull it out to find an envelope addressed, "My Dearest Evelyn…"

I immediately feel my limbs, my mind, my heart go cold. My legs starts to shake, and I grab onto the side of the bed to keep myself from falling. My body is telling me that something isn't right before my mind has a chance to catch up. It has been since the moment I walked into the bedroom.

I take a few deep breaths and shake my head at the overreaction. There could be a million reasons to leave a note. I open the envelope, slowly unfold the letter, and know before I glance at a single word that I have not overreacted. My previous reaction was quite tame for what I was feeling in my soul at this very moment.

My Dearest Evelyn,

> *I have failed you. This is yet another thing I cannot live with myself for. All the good I meant to do for us has only caused more pain. It doesn't matter the good intentions I had when I have added such a layer of fear to our lives. A layer of anxiety that never ceases to attack our minds, my mind. I do not think I can overcome this fear any longer.*
>
> *You did nothing wrong. I know I have treated you as though you have. I only wanted to protect you, to allow you to be the beautiful and brave, strong and loving mother I know you can be. They are your girls now, even Abigail. I know that you will not fail them as I have.*
>
> *I do not believe I can go on carrying the guilt that I hold in my heart, the guilt that rises to the surface every time I look at little Abigail. My late nights are a strain on you. Our home is supposed to be our safe space, but I cannot be there without being overwhelmed by what I have done to you, to us. I am overwhelmed by both the heartache I have caused, and the heartache I feel. None of this is fair to you.*

I pray that you won't find the body, won't see me that way. That no one will. I only want you to remember me as the protector I tried so hard to be. As the one who loved you so deeply, I could not bear to see you suffering or to see you sad. May you now grant me the same kindness in letting me go?

I have set you and the girls up financially so that you may be able to move on, move away. So that you may never suffer the fear and the guilt that plagues me every time I leave the house.

I have also left you another note, one you can give to the police, so that everyone may know what happened to me without knowing why.

Evey, dear, please remember that you did nothing wrong. It is only my fragile mind that can no longer walk the earth with this burden. I will protect you until my very last breath.

Yours Always and Forever,
Scott

I run into the bathroom and throw up. The second letter in the envelope, which I gave to the police, had more information about where he was going. I couldn't bear to read it myself even though I had to make it look as though I had. I just hand it over when they arrived. I keep the other one hidden away in my end table drawer.

A few hours later, I receive word that a body had been found matching Scott's description. They believe he died sometime around late morning. He hadn't even gone into work today.

I couldn't bear to identify him, so a friend of ours did, both of us claiming that I needed to stay with the girls. They still had not woken up – *was this Abby's first time sleeping through the night?* – when the sun shone through the kitchen window the next morning.

The same kitchen window I would stare out of when Scott greeted me every morning.

I make the decision at that very moment to leave. I know that what we did was wrong, but Scott always said it was done to deserving people. Whether he was lying to spare me or speaking the truth, I never allowed myself to think of them as anything other than monsters. It was the only way I could manage my guilt. I had no part in the actual act, so I could dissociate from it a little easier than he could, I suppose.

Perhaps I failed too – failed to protect my husband from the things he had done, the guilt and pain he felt.

I will not fail Rachel and Abby, and I cannot be the mother they need while surrounded by Scott's memories.

Those memories might break me.

CHAPTER 10 – JUNE 2024

RACHEL

I wake up to the sound of my phone ringing and groan. What time is it anyway? I open my eyes to find that I left all the lights on the night before.

I pick up the phone and see 'Detective Cooper' on the screen. I let that go to voicemail. I am not in the mood to talk to anyone, let alone someone calling me at – I look at my phone again – 7:15 in the morning. I haven't even had coffee yet.

I roll over, and the crinkling sound of paper reminds me that I had also fallen asleep with what appears to be my father's suicide note in hand.

Suicide note?

Our mom had always told us that our dad was killed in a car accident. Why would she lie? Is that even what this is? I mean, technically, one could argue that he never used the word "suicide" in the note. I check the date scribbled in the upper right corner of the page. July 11, 2004. That was only a few weeks before we moved from where we lived in Westchester to where we are now.

If it truly is a suicide note, which is what it looks like, why did Abby have it? How long did she have it for, and why would she keep it from me?

It's unfair to feel as hurt and betrayed as I do in this moment, because there may be a perfectly reasonable explanation for this.

I'm starting to feel worse and worse about not hearing Abby out the other day at the coffee shop. I let my anger and hurt over feeling abandoned overshadow the fact that she might really need me, and might be in trouble. If she's really gone, if I never find her, I will never be able to forgive myself.

Panic starts to overcome me as I think about how many days she's been missing. How long do I have to find her? If she's even still...

Stop.

I shake my head. I can't think like that. I will find her. She is going to be alright. Everything is going to be alright.

I'm not quite ready to start the day yet, but I know I can't lay in bed all day with my thoughts running wild either. I need to process what I read, and what I found, before talking to anyone. I get myself out of bed and make my way into the kitchen. I feel my body screaming for caffeine as I get closer to the coffee pot.

I know I'm mentally and physically exhausted from the past few days, but, at some point, I might have to admit that I have a problem when it comes to my need for coffee. Not today, though. Today will not be that day.

I open the cabinet above the coffee pot and find... nothing. I check my pantry for any extra coffee I have stashed for emergencies like this and come up empty.

I groan loudly enough that I wouldn't be surprised if my neighbors came to check on me, then throw myself onto the couch with a loud thump. My thoughts start drifting toward self-pity. Why is absolutely nothing going my way? Why is nothing easy? But I stop myself. That's a dangerous path to go down. It has been weeks since I've been living in this apartment, and I haven't restocked anything since being back. With all the distractions and chaos of the past few days, it hadn't even occurred to me.

I only allow myself to sulk for a few minutes before pulling myself up and getting dressed. I'm going to get coffee, and then I'm going to go for a run. I will probably regret running *after* the coffee, but right now I don't care. Walking to and from the coffee shop might help my body warm up for the run, too.

I pull on my favorite black leggings – the ones with the pockets on the side – and a loose, long-sleeve T-shirt with a cooling material that makes running bearable in the Florida heat. After brushing my teeth, throwing my shoes on, and doing everything else I need to get ready, I set out for J's Coffee Connection.

The walk to the coffee shop is refreshing. The morning sun is bright not too hot yet, and the slight breeze carries the scent of freshly cut grass. It's a small comfort in the midst of everything. By the time I reach the shop, I'm feeling a little more human.

I briefly remember the call from Aiden as I walk, but I push that thought to the back of my mind. I will call him back after my run. I will hopefully have a clearer head then, and he would have called more than once or left a voicemail if it was urgent. In the meantime, I put my headphones in and pick the loudest, most distracting music I have on my phone for my 20-minute walk.

When I finally get to J's, ears ringing, I am greeted at the door by an anxious-looking Jessie holding my usual coffee order.

"I saw you coming from a mile away," she explains gently, as though bracing herself for bad news.

I take the coffee from her as she wraps me in a hug. "Thanks, Jessie."

"How are you, sweetheart?" She starts ushering me to a table as she talks. "I haven't seen you in a few days, and you look like you haven't slept."

"I don't actually think I have slept in the last few days." I laugh to mask the truth in my statement, but Jessie sees through it immediately.

"What's going on? Have you heard from Abigail?"

I shake my head, defeated, unsure where to even start. So much has happened in the past three days — has it only been three days? — and there is nothing in my explanation that won't worry Jessie.

I start from the morning after I was last here. I tell her about my time cleaning out my mom's house, both conversations with Glenn — the normal conversation and the... less normal one — where and how I got robbed, and police involvement. Of course, I leave out specifics about the attractive detective who has been helping me, and I most definitely leave out the text messages.

Finally, I pull the note out of my pocket. I don't know why I brought it with me, but it didn't feel right just leaving it on my dresser. Maybe subconsciously I wanted to share it with someone, with Jessie.

"I just don't know what to make of this. We were always told that Scott, our dad, died in a car accident. This looks like a suicide note."

Jessie takes the note from me, reading it as concern paints her features. When she finishes, she lets out a deep breath. Her only response is a soft nod.

When I don't continue right away, Jessie starts nodding again and says, "It does. It does look just like a suicide note."

"And Abby had it. I don't understand why Abby would have it. Did Mom give it to her? Did she find it and take it? Is that why she got upset and left that day? Why would she not tell me about it either way?" I keep asking the questions as though someone will have the answers. No one does.

I feel myself starting to hyperventilate again and reach for my coffee just to have something in my hands to keep them steady.

"Breathe, Rach. Breathe." I know I'm starting to get hysterical, and that's not what I came here for.

"I'm sorry." I feel the tears coming as my voice cracks on the last word. I need to stop that. People are going to start thinking I am mentally unstable.

"You have nothing to be sorry for, dear." Jessie moves her chair then, so instead of sitting across from me, she is now sitting by my side. She wraps her arms around me, and, just before the tears start falling, she asks in a soft voice, "Did you know I was married?"

I wipe a single escaped tear, look up at her in shock, and shake my head. We have known Jessie for a few years now. She is like a mom to everyone who knows her, but she never had any children of her own. Abby and I always assumed she just never married.

"Oh yes. Probably before you were even born. I was married very young, nineteen years old. My husband, Owen, always told me he fell in love with me from the moment he laid his eyes on me. We met when we were 4." She laughs to herself then, recalling a faraway memory that only she could ever truly feel, that only she has the privilege of remembering now. "I always used to roll my eyes when he said that, and when he said things like he never wanted to live a second of this life without me, the corny stuff. Of course, I felt the same at the time."

"Did those feelings change?" I interject.

Jessie pauses then, looking as though she were holding back tears of her own. "No, dear. Never. Nineteen years old and this man did everything I could ever ask of another person. He loved me so fiercely. I couldn't fathom anyone else loving another person as much as he loved me. He was a person who felt every emotion so deeply. I think that's what made losing him the hardest. 6 years after we were married, he committed suicide. He never left a note, just left me to find him. I never told anyone who didn't absolutely need to know. I was embarrassed. Not by him, of course. Never by him. I was embarrassed because I should have known. He felt everything so deeply, but he only showed the good emotions, never the bad. I never even knew he was struggling. I felt ashamed of myself."

Endless tears are streaming down my face. I'm not sobbing or shaking anymore, but the tears keep spilling over as I stare at Jessie, unsure of how to proceed with the conversation.

Before I can come up with anything to contribute, Jessie continues. "I tell you all this only to say that your mother, sweet Evelyn, well she may have been protecting herself by not telling you girls the truth. Now, I have no idea why she would tell little Abigail and not you. Maybe those answers will come in time. I just mean it might do you some good to give your mother a little grace on this one."

My mind spun. Protecting herself? Was she ashamed? Or was there truly something within this family that needed to be hidden? I don't feel as sure as I did before. She told Abby something that day in the hospital that may have somehow led to her running off, although that's still up for debate, but Abby wouldn't have run off because of a suicide note, right? If that's even when Mom told her about this note. If she even told Abby about it at all.

"Thank you, Jessie. For everything, truly." I wrap my arms around her in a hug that lasts several minutes before we are interrupted by the loud chirp of my phone ringing. I check the caller ID and see Detective Cooper's name pop up on the screen once again. I feel my sigh through my whole body. I shoot Jessie an "I'm sorry" glance and answer the phone.

Jessie waves off my apology and walks back over to the counter, giving me the space she knows I need for this. I pick up my coffee and head to the table I normally designate as mine and Abby's, but it allows for more privacy being tucked in the back corner the way it is.

"Hi, Detective?" I question, though I know who it is already.

"Aiden."

"Aiden," I parrot, tone and all, as I try and fail to not roll my eyes.

"Why didn't you call me back earlier?" His tone sounds sharp, urgent, and my stomach drops.

"I needed coffee first," I reply, matter-of-fact.

"You didn't think I might've had something important to say?"

"I figured if you had found Abby, you would blow up this phone until I answered. Anything else could wait until after I had my coffee. I had a rough night."

Aiden sighs so loud through the phone that I imagine him reaching through and physically shaking me. I can practically see him shaking his head and pinching the bridge of his nose. I stop for a second to wonder how I had gotten so familiar with his habits in just a few days. I shudder and derail that train of thought before I start down that rabbit hole.

"Okay," he finally starts again. "Are you able to talk now?"

"Yes."

"Where did you say you moved here from?"

Right into questioning, I guess. "Why?"

"Can you just answer the question please." His tone today is immediately putting me on edge. He sounds like a completely different person from the one I sat talking to for an hour at my sister's kitchen table yesterday.

"Am I being interrogated here or something?" I don't want to sound rude or defensive, but I refuse to sit here and be interrogated again when he should be focusing his energy on actually finding Abby.

"No, no. I'm sorry." He softens his tone, and I let out a breath I didn't realize I was holding. Just like that, he sounds like the guy from yesterday. "No, I'm just trying to connect some dots here. My police voice comes out without my permission sometimes."

"Apology accepted." I pause. "A little town outside of Miami called Westchester."

"And when did you say you moved here?"

"Why?" I ask again.

"Connecting dots, remember? I'll explain in a second — I just want to make sure I'm not reaching first."

"August 2004. Right before I started Kindergarten."

"Oh." Does he sound… defeated?

"Why?" I say, more demanding this time.

"Your sister, Abigail Stephens. I told you that she's legally on record as deceased."

"Yes, we've gone over this. I told you that I'm not crazy, she is alive, and she is missing." I let out a huff.

"Yes, and I told you I believe you. Not the point," he scolds me.

"Sorry, continue."

"The date of her death is listed as April 3, 2003. However, and this is the part I don't understand, that record was just updated four days ago. The day you said you saw her, and the day she presumably went missing." He hears my protest before I even start, and he quickly adds, "I'm not blaming, and I'm not insinuating. I'm giving you a timeline."

"Okay, continue." I only pause for a minute before… "Wait, someone changed her record of death?" I say this louder than I mean to and take a quick look around to make sure I didn't attract any attention with my outburst.

"I can't see the changes that have been made, but yes. It looks like someone made a change, or changes, four days ago. Why that record would have been changed, I have no idea."

"Okay, and what does this have to do with where I used to live?" I question, struggling to follow where he's trying to go with this.

"Last night, a missing person's case from April 6, 2002, was also changed from pending to resolved. Have you ever heard the name Victoria Wright?"

I sit with the name for a minute, my mind reaching for some forgotten memory or dream where I might've heard that name before. Not coming up with anything, I respond, "No, should I have?"

"I suppose not. You were young when she was taken, obviously, but she was a 1-year-old little girl who went missing in the Miami area in April 2003. The case was never solved and Victoria was never found. Until now. At least according to our system. No one has any real confirmation that Victoria Wright is alive. Or any idea why that would've been changed or who would've changed it. There hasn't been anything in the local or national news to suggest she's been reunited with her family. Nothing on social media. Simply nothing."

"So, you're saying…?" I still feel like I'm missing some bigger point here.

"I don't really know because the dates don't line up anyway. At the risk of being yelled at, I was wondering if your parents might've had any involvement in something here. Maybe they knew the family? Just the timing of your sister's supposed death, the kidnapping, both records being changed in the same week…"

"Well, my dad has been dead almost 20 years, and I buried my mom less than a week ago, so I don't think they're changing any police records," I bite out. I react exactly how he was afraid I was going to react, and the guilt starts forming a knot in my stomach. I need to ease up.

Aiden doesn't flinch at my tone, keeping his as gentle as ever. "I know. You're right. I am reaching, which is precisely what I was trying not to do. I'm just trying to find any connection, any information that might lead to finding your sister." He pauses like he wants to say more but doesn't.

"Well, I appreciate your help, and your belief in me thus far."

After You're Gone

"That's sort of the other thing." His tone changes again, like he's... upset? Scared?

"What other thing?"

"I can't actually help on police time anymore. I'm being told that I'm wasting, quote, 'precious tax dollars' working a clear runaway case. My boss is really on my back about it, and I need to drop the case for now."

"You know she's not a runaway. She's in trouble!" I feel my blood boiling and my face turning red as I start to lose control of the volume of my voice. Why even bother speaking to me about any of this if he is just going to drop it?

"I know, I'm..."

"Don't even say you're sorry." I cut him off. "Thanks for everything, Detective Cooper." I spit the last two words at him and hang the phone up.

I down the rest of my coffee in one gulp and walk the cup back up to the counter.

"Everything okay?" Jessie asks concern back in her eyes.

"Yes, nothing new to report," I lie. I don't know how to explain what Aiden was trying to connect, and I don't want to think about it anymore. No use giving his new theory any voice if he isn't willing to help sort out the details and doesn't think he has anything of substance.

"Do you want a coffee for the road?"

"Thanks, Jessie. I walked here, and I think I'm going to go for a run right from here." I motion to the workout clothes and smile sheepishly at her. "I need to clear my head."

"Alright, sweetie. Well, you know where to find me if you need me."

"Thank you for everything." I try to convey how meaningful our conversation was for me with my expression, positive that neither of us want everyone here to know what we discussed.

She nods, letting me know she understands, and I begin my walk to the start of the trail behind my apartment.

I run for about an hour. There is a beautiful trail that wraps around my neighborhood. It passes a few different ponds before opening up to the ocean. Growing up so close to the water has always been a blessing. Living in an environment surrounded by water has always been the most calming thing for me, though I sometimes wonder if I would have always felt that way or if the proximity created the comfort. The wildlife everywhere is fun to watch, too. Seeing the occasional alligator or birds that stand as tall as I do never gets old.

As I circle back to my apartment building, I see his car before I see him. The police cruiser parked directly behind my car is unmistakable and part of me wants to turn and run in the other direction as soon as I lay eyes on it. I had turned my phone on silent during my run and, checking it now, I see that I have several missed calls from him. I sigh, knowing it is better to face him and get rid of him now than to try to hide forever.

As I approach my door, I see the man sitting in front of it fidgeting with his fingers while he waits for me to return.

"How did you know where I lived?"

He startles. Good. "Uh, you gave me your address, your information, when you filed that missing person's report. Happy belated birthday, by the way. I missed that before."

I manage to stop myself from rolling my eyes. "Are police allowed to use that information to stalk the person filing said report?"

His face turns bright red, and I watch him physically cringe. He is embarrassed, and I almost feel bad for making him that uncomfortable.

"No, no. I uh... I'm not stalking. That's such an awful word. God, no, that's not what I'm doing." I wait for him to finish stumbling over his words. I know that feeling well and decide to take it a little easier on him. At least, I will once I figure out why he's here. "Listen, everything I said on the phone at the end – I'm not giving up on you. I'm not saying I believe that this is a runaway case. Christ, I was up half the night last night trying to connect imaginary dots. I just mean I cannot work on this on police time." He emphasizes the words 'on police time' like I missed something obvious when he said these words earlier.

He rises from where he is sitting on my doorstep as he speaks, and I take in his distinctly not-cop look. He has on a pair of washed-out jeans and a light blue V-neck that screams casual-cool. Because of how lean and generally fit he looks, it isn't hard to picture what he looks like under his uniform. However, the shirt he wears now is practically glued to his torso, and you can clearly see every line of his sculpted muscles. His dark brown spikes from the other day are falling in his face now, a little shaggier than before, as though he only combs through it on the days he works.

I definitely prefer this look.

"So, what does that mean?" I ask, trying not to stutter myself.

"That means I can take a leave of absence for a bit in order to help you." His cautious look turns into a wide grin, as though he would love nothing more than to offer this extended version of his help.

I start shaking my head before he can continue, and his grin falters slightly. There is absolutely no reason this man should take time off work or risk his job or career or self to help me.

"...Or I can help you on off hours," he perks up again.

"Why are you helping me at all?" I can't help but ask the question.

"Well, aside from the fact that it is my job to help people, and it's why I got into this profession in the first place, I just have a feeling that something isn't right here. Call it a gut feeling, I guess, but my gut is usually correct. And with everything you've been through, you deserve some proper answers."

I just nod, because I don't know what else to say.

After a silence that lasts too long, Aiden asks, "So, can I come in so we can finish our talk?"

I do my best to hide my shock. He means help *now* and a warm feeling starts in my chest. A feeling I am only going to associate with gratitude.

"There's more to talk about?"

"I think we should go over the details again, figure out if we can come up with any theories. You're my only partner now, remember." He says this as though he can think of nothing better. As though he believes it's an honor to be my partner, not the other way around.

I laugh at the absurdity of his last statement but move to unlock my door. "It's a bit of a disaster, and I don't have any coffee, so I apologize in advance."

We enter the apartment, and I follow his gaze. I wonder what he could be thinking, what he is judging, why I care. Every little mess seems bigger, every spot on the counter seems dirtier than when I was looking at it with my own eyes.

I grow self-conscious in record time, which reminds me that I am also a mess. I feel sweaty and gross from my run, and now I can't think about anything but cleaning myself up for the distinctly-not-a-mess guy standing in my doorway.

"Would you mind watching TV for a few minutes? I just got back from a run, and I could use a quick shower."

"Sure, no problem. Take your time." He waves me off as he moves to sit on the couch.

"Okay. Can I get you a water or anything?"

"Don't worry about me. I can manage for a few minutes." The short laugh that follows as he takes a seat is musical. I grab a change of clothes and race into my bathroom before my heart melts completely.

Get your shit together, I scold myself internally and make a mental note to call Kara. She'll talk some sense into me.

In the meantime, I argue with myself for the full five minutes about what it means that he's in my apartment right now. Does he offer to take a leave of absence on every case he gets told to drop? Does he make house calls? Maybe the answer to both is yes, or maybe this hasn't happened to him before.

Either way, I don't think this is completely normal. With him looking the way he does, especially in that t-shirt, my thoughts head down a path of *hoping* he doesn't make house calls for just anyone. I start to picture him waiting on my couch, in what is practically my bedroom, and…

Nope.

This is completely inappropriate. He is only here to help me find Abby.

Stepping out of the shower, I dry off and change into the clothes I brought into the bathroom. When I walk out to my kitchen to grab myself a water, I expect to see Aiden on the couch, playing on his phone or locked into some true crime TV show. Instead, I stop short, finding him staring at all the pictures on my wall.

"What are you doing?"

He startles again, and I crack up laughing this time. This is becoming prime entertainment for me.

When we both compose ourselves, he points to one of the pictures on the wall and asks who the girl is. I walk over next to him to get a better look at the picture he's asking about. "That's Kara and me. We were just starting high school there." I point to the one next to it. "And that's Abby and me the night she graduated high school. And that's Abby, mom, and me out in mom's garden." I can hear the hint of nostalgia in my voice that I know he doesn't understand, but I can't find it in myself to hold it back.

Out of the corner of my eyes, I see him looking right at me, and I immediately grow self-conscious again. Cheeks now flushed, I move over to the couch and sit down, patting the seat next to me. "Let's get talking!"

He follows and takes the seat nearest to where my hand just was. Not close enough to make me uncomfortable but closer than I thought he would.

"So first, I want to apologize for upsetting you on the phone earlier. Obviously, that part of the conversation did not go as planned. That being said, something about this is not adding up. I've never gotten this much flack for taking a case that 'may lead nowhere.'" He motions his fingers to make air quotes. "I'm not a believer in coincidences. Most of the time, there's an explanation or a reason for everything. And when there isn't, it's usually because we haven't found that reasoning yet."

I nod, helping him along past his philosophical theories.

"Anyway, these are the events as I see it. One, your mom gets sick and your sister runs away for months after a conversation they had. Two, your sister comes back after your mom dies, after the funeral, and needs to tell you something. Three, she can't be reached for days after that and gets reported missing."

"Yep, that about sums it up."

"Okay, and we have no idea what might have been said in that conversation, right?"

"Well..." I hesitate, contemplating showing him the note or not. Based on the way he's looking at me now though, I have to give him something. "This really could be nothing. And this by itself isn't a good enough reason to make Abby run away. I would also like to point out that I have no idea when she got this, so again, it could mean absolutely nothing."

It's his turn to motion for me to hurry up, to get to the point. I stand up to find the leggings I had on earlier and retrieve the note from the pocket. I hand it to Aiden, explaining, "My mom always told us our dad, Scott, was killed in a car accident one month before we moved here. July of 2004." I sigh, holding back tears I should not have left in me. "I found this at Abby's house yesterday, in her suitcase."

"Yesterday, like when I found you there?"

I nod.

"And you didn't think to mention it?"

"Well, I didn't read it until I got home last night, so I didn't know what it was. And I didn't know if I could trust you yet," I shrug my shoulders. That reasoning sounds good enough to me.

"Fair enough."

He takes what feels like forever to read the note. At some point, I sit back down on the couch next to him, biting my nails as I lock my gaze on his face. Finally, he lets out a long breath and says, "This is a suicide note."

His tone is matter-of-fact. He isn't asking. Still, I answer, "Yes, it seems so."

"And Abby had this?"

"Well, it was in her suitcase in the pouch on the inside."

"And you think your mom might've given this to her when she left before?"

"I don't know. I don't know why she would've given it to Abby and not me, or not at least told me about it. That's what I don't understand. I also don't feel like that by itself is enough to make her run away for months with hardly any communication."

"You don't think Abby would have some extreme reaction to finding this out? Has she ever reacted to any news like this before?"

"We've never really gotten news like this before, but no. She wasn't a person to just run away from issues. That was always me, and she was always the one grounding me, bringing me back to reality. The whole thing is so out of character for her. That's why there either has to be more to this than the note, or the note is completely unrelated. She may have needed a breather, but she wouldn't have abandoned me over this. And she wouldn't have kept this from me under normal circumstances."

"Do you think this had something to do with what she was trying to tell you the other day?"

"You mean when I wouldn't give her the time of day?" I let out a self-deprecating laugh.

"It's not your fault."

"I'm not so sure about that." I shake my head, not in the mood to be talked out of any self-loathing at the moment.

"Maybe she's been taken to keep her quiet about whatever it is she found out. Maybe, if she had told you, you'd both be missing now, and there would be no one to find either of you."

"That's a little extreme don't you think?"

"I'm trained to plan for the worst-case scenarios. And, unfortunately, I've seen worse theories come to light," he admits, apologetically.

In need of a breather myself and realizing I never did get the water I wanted, I stand and walk into the kitchen, grabbing a water from the refrigerator. "Want one?" I wave the water bottle I have in my hand.

"Sure."

Handing Aiden the bottle, I let out a sigh as I fall back down onto the couch.

"I don't know. I just feel like I failed her. I wasn't there when she needed me. I know what you're going to say, but it doesn't matter that she wasn't there for me. I know deep down that she has her reasons. We're sisters. We don't keep score. I failed her when it mattered, and now I may never see her again."

"You had a fair reaction, though. How could you have known that you wouldn't have an opportunity to make it up to her the next day?" he says, desperately trying to absolve me from any perceived wrongdoing. I don't understand why he's trying so hard.

I stay silent for a while, not wanting to continue arguing my guilt. I can't continue to listen to him trying to console me either, so a short break from both is necessary.

After a few minutes of silence that Aiden doesn't try to break, I remember another piece of the puzzle we're discussing. "There is probably something else I should show you."

He waits for me to explain impatiently, his leg bouncing up and down.

I pull out my phone and show him the two messages I have from the blocked number. His face goes white faster than I expected. Maybe I should have told him about these sooner.

He is frozen in place long enough that I'm about to check for a pulse, to make sure he is still breathing, when he urgently demands, "Who has this number?"

"No one. You and Kara, that's it. And I don't know if cashier's who sell these things can hack into them, but they know I have the phone. I was with Kara when I got the first one. It was a few hours after I had gotten the phone. And I'm pretty sure, I hope, that I can trust you. Especially now that I've shown you these. So…"

"And you didn't show me these sooner because…?" he asks, clearly annoyed.

"Again, because I didn't know I *could* trust you. You were the only other person who had this number."

"Okay. Right. And, no. As far as the cashiers go, that's highly unlikely and very illegal." He softens his tone. With a slight hesitation, he asks, "So, you trust me now?" The way he asks, the way he looks at me, I know I can. I know he wasn't asking for some confirmation that didn't matter. There is no 'hunter ensuring his prey is firmly in the trap' in his question. He has nothing to do with whatever is going on here. Only genuine concern for my opinion of him. Maybe it's easier for him to work when people feel they can believe in him, and so it's an instinctual thing for him to seek out the trust of other people.

Either way, he's done enough, shown me enough, to have earned my trust now. So, I give it to him.

"I do."

A nod and the ghost of a smile lets me know he appreciates the trust I'm giving him and that he wouldn't let that trust go to waste.

Switching gears, he asks, "Did you respond to these?"

"No."

"And when did the second one come in?"

"Late last night. When I was finishing up at my mom's house."

"Did you see anyone yesterday?

"Yes. My old neighbor, Glenn. I was… sort of breaking down in my car, in my mom's driveway. He's always outside watering his plants or whatever, so I guess he saw me and tried to help me feel better."

"And did he?"

"Not really." I watch Aiden's face and see something there I don't like. "No, no, no. Glenn watched us grow up. His wife was best friends with my mom before she passed away a few years ago. We spent all our weekends together, did everything for each other. He would never hurt Abby or me. Never."

"Okay, I believe you." He throws his arms up in mock surrender.

"He was acting strange yesterday. More aggressively asking about Abby and if I had seen her. I never even told him she came back a few days ago. It was weird. But I think he was just worried about her. Like I said, this is unlike her. And to miss the funeral…" I trail off, shaking my head. "I did leave feeling a little unsettled, but I think it was just a combination of both our moods. I was only with him a few minutes and then spent the rest of the day cleaning out my mom's place."

"Maybe there's something in your mom's place that someone doesn't want you to find?"

"Maybe," I shrug, unconvinced.

We talk around in circles for another half hour, walking through everyone Abby and I both knew, going over the timeline of when we moved, the dates that were changed in the system and when, and walking through my last couple of days again.

We are getting nowhere.

Finally, he pauses, checking the time.

"Are you getting hungry at all? I've taken up your whole day. The least I could do is get us a pizza."

Pizza actually sounds amazing, but I am overwhelmed with everything we have been discussing. I need some time alone to process this.

"Look, I really appreciate you coming over. I just need to sit with all of this for a bit. Clear my head."

He takes the rejection like a pro which only makes me fonder of him but also makes me feel worse about the mild rejection. Still, I help him gather all his notes, and he heads toward the door.

"Rachel, if you need anything at all, I'm on your side. I just want you to know that I'm here to help, and I want to find your sister. Just don't call the station anymore. Here is my cell number, so use that from now on whenever you need anything." He hands me a card with a phone number scribbled on it and wraps me in an unexpected hug. The shock of that feeling keeps me still for a few seconds too long before I wrap my arms around him in return.

I manage to wait until he leaves before my cheeks heat up again.

I take my phone out of my pocket and call Kara before I lose the nerve to hear the truth. It rings a few times before going to voicemail.

Weird. Kara always answers.

At the tone, I say, "Kara. Major detective issues! I might have a *crush* which sounds so, so high school and is also very wrong! Please call me back so you can talk me out of this! I also have some updates on everything else going on. Okay, love you!"

Hopefully, she will call back soon.

It's a few hours later when I receive another text.

I PRAY YOU WON'T FIND THE BODY. YOU DID NOTHING WRONG. YOU WERE JUST TRYING TO BE ABBY'S PROTECTOR. BUT I TOLD YOU TO STOP.

CHAPTER 11 – JUNE 2024

RACHEL

I throw the phone across the room.

I'm not breathing for a few seconds too long and find myself gasping for air when I manage to start again.

THE BODY?!?!?

So many alarm bells go off at once.

Who is sending these messages? The body? Abby's body? Why would I not want to find… I can't even bring myself to finish that thought. Abby is still alive. I just have to find her.

Abby's protector? What does that even mean? Because I've been looking for her? Of course, I want to protect her.

After a few more minutes of spiraling, it occurs to me that there is no threat in this text message. Maybe saying "the body" was supposed to be a threat, but the other messages were a direct threat towards me. Why is this one different?

I quickly throw out my theory of 'cashier messing with me' even though Aiden threw that out for me a few hours ago. No random cashier would know my sister's name, and this feels too…strange… to be a practical joke.

Along another train of thought, my mind races back to something Aiden said earlier. Maybe there is something at the house, and whoever is sending the text messages knows that. I don't, for one second, believe my mom has anything to do with this. But Aiden made a good point about the timing of everything and how I got that second text about snooping right after leaving my mom's house.

I need to stop and breathe and think. I have so many questions and practically no answers.

Is this last text actually different, or am I grasping at straws? Most likely grasping, I quickly conclude.

Could there be something at the house that would give me a clue as to what happened to Abby? There's really only one way to find out.

I debate what I should do next. Call Aiden? Go to the house to look for clues, if they even exist? I'll start with driving to my mom's house and go from there. I can call Kara on the way to fill her in and hopefully, she can help me think straight. Hopefully, she'll answer this time.

I grab my keys and wallet off the kitchen counter and a denim jacket off the hook on the wall next to the front door. As I am walking out, I remember Scott's note. I still don't want to let that note out of my sight. It's the only thing in all of this I realistically have to grasp onto.

The drive to the house isn't long, so I call Kara right away. Still no answer. That's odd. It's late, and she should be done working by now. I leave another voicemail expressing how urgent my most recent information feels and to meet me at my mom's house as soon as she can.

I'm almost at the house when I get a callback.

"Hey Kara!" I answer. "Are you still working? Did you listen to my voicemails? Ignore the fir-"

"Hi, Rachel." She cuts me off, her voice lacking all emotion. I'm taken aback by her lack of concern, especially if she did, in fact, hear them. "Listen, I really think that it's a good idea for you to leave this alone now."

What?

"Leave this alone? Are you crazy? This is Abigail. You know, your friend, my sister, missing?"

"I know. And if she still hasn't made an appearance or tried to contact you, this is really a matter for the police. Not you. Maybe she really did just run off again and doesn't want to be bothered."

I start to argue, but she cuts me off. "Rach, this is dangerous." The words sound like they should be coming from someone who cares, but her tone is cold. "You need to calm down. Let the police handle it, or this will get worse for *all* of us."

"Kara, what are you even talking about. You're not making any sense."

"If you are truly my friend, and you want to *protect* us, you will leave this alone. That's the only way to *protect* us."

Before I have a chance to react, she hangs up the phone. It takes me a few seconds before I register the last thing she said. The emphasis she placed on the last few words…

If you want to protect us. The only way to protect us…

Protect? Basically, the same word that was used in the last text message. Is it a coincidence?

In all the years I've known Kara, she has never once sounded like that, never once spoke to me in that way. It's like it wasn't even Kara speaking. There was no feeling in her voice, no concern for Abby, for me. Nothing. It terrified me.

I also remember another point Aiden made. No one but him and Kara had my new phone number. And if he wasn't the one sending the texts…

No. There is absolutely no way she is behind this. What reason would she have to be behind Abby missing? She would never hurt a living soul, let alone her two best friends.

And yet, something doesn't feel right.

That word 'protect' continues to gnaw at me. It's like a movie quote you've heard a million times but you can never place the movie it's from, so you just let the line drive you crazy.

Protect. Protect. Protect.

Why is that word sticking out in my mind? Kara said it twice with so much emphasis which makes me think…

Protect…

Protect…or.

The note.

Realization hits me like a freight train.

Even though I'm only two minutes away from the house at this point, I pull over to the side of the road. I take the suicide note out of my jacket pocket, thanking every lucky star in existence that I've been keeping it with me, and reread it along with the text message.

I pray you won't find the body.

You did nothing wrong.

Protector.

All lines from our dad's note. All part of the text message.

I knew there was something different about the last text. I could feel it.

Suddenly, the news about "Abby's death" and the kidnapping back in Westchester doesn't feel out of place. The supposed suicide happened while we were all still in Westchester. I can only assume the "protector" hints came from Kara because she's with Abby. How else would Kara know to reference that note?

If these are the only clues I'm ever going to get, then I have to believe they point to Westchester. To the house, or at least the area all of these clues come from.

Could Abby really be missing because of something that happened when we were kids?

I begin to feel like maybe Aiden was talking about the wrong house when he implied that there could be clues connected to Abby's disappearance. We moved out of that house in Westchester so Evelyn could escape her grief, but maybe she wanted to escape more than just grief. Maybe it was a reminder of something that happened there.

I settle on my plan but know I need to stop at the house first. At Mom's house yesterday, I found a box and a filing cabinet filled with old papers and have the feeling I can find an address somewhere in there. Maybe in an old bill or in some record of the sale of the house, I'm not sure. Some of those folders had years on them from before we moved here, and that's where I'm going to start.

It takes almost two hours sorting through documents to find one that has anything to do with our old house. When I finally do, I put the address into my phone and map from where I'm at in Bradenton. Just under 4 hours, and it is highway practically the whole way.

Checking the time, I see it's just before midnight, which means I'll be up driving all night if I leave now. I don't imagine I'll be getting any sleep tonight either way, and I want to get moving as soon as possible, so I head out.

I call Aiden while I fill up my gas tank at the station down the street. I don't think he'll let me go tonight without some kind of argument concerning my safety, but if Kara really is up to something, or I do find something at the old house, I need somebody to be on my side.

When the call goes to voicemail, I feel both a sense of frustration and a wave of relief. Does nobody answer their phone anymore? At least I avoid a lecture and him trying to talk me out of my plan for now.

When I hear his voice asking the caller to leave a message, I explain Kara's phone call, the text message I got a few hours before, and the connections I made. Deciding I can't do much more than that, I hang up the phone and start driving.

Music, always the best distraction, is doing absolutely nothing to take my mind off of everything on this too-long drive, but I can't drive nearly 4 hours in silence. I try all my playlists, from hard rock to 90s throwback music. Even my favorite bands can't pull me out of my intrusive thoughts. They consistently drift to what could possibly be waiting for me.

The switch to podcasts doesn't help either. It's going to be a long drive.

About halfway into the drive, Aiden finally calls me, pure panic in his voice.

"Hey, Rachel. I'm so sorry I missed your call earlier. Just wait for me – I'll go with you. It might not be safe."

"Hi, Aiden. You know, it's…" I check the clock, "…2 A.M. Why are you even up? I wasn't expecting you to go with me. I'm already halfway there."

I hear a loud groan and then a noisy racket, like a bunch of pens falling off a desk. Ignoring the question about his sleeping habits, he starts, "Rachel, if what you're saying is true, you have no idea what you're getting yourself into. You could be dealing with very dangerous people."

"How do you know there will even be people there?" I say, getting defensive.

"I don't, but what if there are?"

"Well, then I think I can handle myself." I sigh. "We haven't lived there in over 20 years. The house was sold. There's a new family living there that has nothing to do with mine. I'm sure it's a dead end. I just don't know what else to do."

"And you're going to, what? Show up on this new family's doorstep at 4 in the morning? What's the plan?"

"Well, no. I just want to scope the place out for a bit. I'll go back in the morning to talk to them. See if they've seen or heard anything strange."

"That's a terrible plan." I can hear the frustration, the eye roll in his voice.

"I don't know what else to do. It's the only information I have." I'm starting to sound desperate, and I hate that I'm coming off as weak. I find myself caring more and more about whether or not *he* thinks I'm weak, which is ridiculous. "Look, I'll be fine. If it will make you feel better, I can check in with you. But I have to do this. If this is somehow connected to that note, Abby had that note for who knows how long. She could be reaching out to me the only way she knows how. I'm going." My tone left no room for argument.

"Fine," he surrenders. "It's not like I can do anything to stop you anyway considering you're halfway there. Text me as soon as you get there and let me know how it all looks." He sounds beyond exasperated.

"I will," I promise.

"Be safe, please," he says, before hanging up the phone.

Maybe it was the time, the lack of sleep, the adrenaline, but I found myself replaying the way he said be *safe* over and over in my head. I start convincing myself that he cares about what happens to me while also reminding myself that he is just working. I continue going back and forth, and it turns out to be a better distraction than anything else I've tried so far.

I really need to get out more.

Two hours later, I pull up to the street I grew up on.

The street I'm supposed to turn onto, according to my GPS, isn't a neighborhood at all. It's hard to get a real feel for the life of this street in the middle of the night, but I have vague memories of walking around a neighborhood that doesn't quite match with what

I see now. It's just one long street lined with houses. Then again, when you're 4 years old, I'm sure everything looks a little vaster and details start to blur as you get older.

Even at nearly 4 in the morning, I can see the street does have the potential to be neighborly. All of the houses look well taken care of for an older neighborhood, decorations line the three-pane window in the front of every house. Evidence of kids running around during the day can be seen in the chalk on the sidewalk and the bikes left in the front yard. More evidence of a close-knit, neighborly community is found when I realize the street comes to an end.

My headlights catch the street signs that signal a dead end, as some tightly locked away memory of block parties and gatherings try to resurface. There are two grills sitting just behind the signs in the grass, and picnic tables set up behind the grills. It looks like the community set up a makeshift park at the end of the street.

I look down at my GPS and see that the house I'm looking for is the last house on the right.

I feel instant recognition when I pull up but no real familiarity. This house is the house I spent the first few years of my life in, but I don't have any immediate feelings of warmth, fond memories, or *home*. It's almost as though I dreamt this house up years ago, knew everything about the house I created in my mind, but lost some detail, some feeling, upon waking up. I was now staring at a manifestation of this fragmented dream.

The contradiction between what I know and what I feel is jarring.

Still, I don't fully know what to expect. The place isn't exactly run down – the lawn has been clearly maintained, and the place looks intact. However, the shutters on either side of the front windows look grimy, there are shingles missing from the roof, there is no décor in the windows or on the front step as I saw in the other homes I passed. I don't see any cars in the driveway, either. Something about the house feels lifeless compared to the others.

Maybe the people who live here just don't care about being neighborly. We all know people like that, I guess. My mind conjures up an image of Abby's nosy neighbor, and I shudder.

It could also be that the night is throwing off my vision and my senses. Either way, I know I can't stay parked here. If there is anyone in that house, I don't want them watching me stalk the place.

I turn the car around at the end of the road and park a few houses down. I want to let Aiden know I made it, if only because of how concerned he seemed.

Made it to the house. Seems off – looks abandoned. Going to get a hotel and come back in a few hours.

I definitely want to check the house out more and talk to whoever lives here.

If anyone, I can't help finishing the thought.

However, I'm not stupid enough to attempt a breaking and entering in the middle of the night to find out just how unoccupied the house is, and I certainly am not going to knock on the door and disturb anyone who might be sleeping.

I search on my phone for hotels nearby and find the only one within 10 minutes that doesn't have reviews of roaches or bed bugs. I plug the address into my GPS and head in that direction.

CHAPTER 12 – JUNE 2024

RACHEL

My alarm goes off at 6 in the morning. In my groggy, sleep-deprived state, it's a minute before my eyes adjust and I remember where I'm at. A dingy hotel not too far outside of Miami, only a few minutes from the house I'm here to investigate.

This hotel doesn't feel like anything more than a motel with indoor rooms. With a short hallway and a small office desk for a lobby, no breakfast area or little shop filled with common forgotten toiletries and snacks, and rooms that look like they haven't been updated since the 1950s, I have certainly stayed in nicer places.

However, when you're in an unfamiliar area in the middle of the night, you don't have much in the way of options. At least, true to reviews, I didn't see any bugs.

The sun isn't up yet, but I know it will be soon. I want to get back to the neighborhood a little before daylight and check the place out again before I go knocking on any doors. For now, I have enough time to get dressed and ready, not that there is much I can do in terms of cleaning up. I want to take a shower, but one look at the bathroom and the free toiletries by the sink has me throwing my hair in a ponytail and splashing water on my face. Even the hand towels smell musty.

Yeah, showering when I get home is a much better option.

If I get home.

I shake the thought out of my head.

I pull on my jeans and t-shirt from the day before, officially the new theme of my life, and make a mental note to pack a small bag of essentials to leave in my car at all times in case I ever need to leave quickly in the middle of the night again.

Before leaving, I check my phone for any messages or updates from Aiden. Nothing. He was more than likely already asleep when I texted him before and just hasn't gotten up yet. I will call him if I come across anything that seems important. Otherwise, I can't afford to worry about him right now.

I grab what little I have in the room and head out. The sun is just starting to peek over the horizon, but I might still be able to find a place to park under the camouflage of the dark if I hurry. I check the map on my phone to get an idea of the house's immediate surroundings and see a park one block over. If there is a parking lot there — and why wouldn't there be? — it looks like I can park there and walk. The map shows a small patch of wooded area between the park and the street signs I saw at the dead end of the road.

When I pull up to the park, I find nothing more than a metal slide, a swing set with two worn-out swings, and a rusty see-saw all sitting on a bed of wood chips. There were only three parking spaces, but it looks as though this park has long been abandoned. A bad afternoon thunderstorm could take out these metal death traps. Hopefully, my car won't get towed.

Unfortunately, it doesn't look like there is a clear path connecting the park to the neighborhood, likely because it doesn't get used very often. The area of trees is small enough that it's easy to navigate. I have walked through denser, more dangerous woods.

As I start walking, though, it becomes clear that the lack of sunlight puts me at a disadvantage. There are tree roots sticking up out of the ground, and I can't avoid them all. I'm just thankful that I am almost always in sneakers.

I reach the sidewalk at the front of the house and start to walk towards the front door when I notice a woman, not much older than my mom had been, pushing a stroller in my direction.

Continuing my walk up the sidewalk, I jump when I hear a voice say, "No one's there, ma'am."

Startled by the voice, I turn to face the woman as she closes the distance between us. "Excuse me?"

"No one's lived there for nearly twenty years now. Some woman with her children moved out right after her husband died. No one's been back to this house since." A distinctly southern drawl and calm demeanor has the opposite effect of what I would normally expect.

I'm sure this woman is just trying to be helpful, but I also don't know her from a hole in the wall. I'm not taking any chances when it comes to finding Abby.

"So, you're saying this house has been sitting here empty for the last twenty years? No one else ever moved in or out?" I don't hide the skepticism I'm feeling.

"Been here basically my whole life, ma'am. Never seen anyone else in or out of this house. The troubled couple, they were. The best thing for that woman was to leave with those girls."

Great. We were the town's gossip for twenty years, and Abby and I never even heard the real story.

"This house was sold by that woman, though. You're saying those buyers never moved in?"

"Don't know what to tell ya. Never seen no one else in or out of that house. Just tryin' ta save you some trouble, ma'am. I hope you have a nice rest of your day."

With a wave, she turns the stroller she is pushing and walks away.

"You, too! Thanks for the help!" I shout after her, but she doesn't acknowledge me. I'm not sure I even believe the woman. I have seen the documents for the sale of the house. Unless they were fake, or unless those people never moved in, someone else had to have lived here for at least some time. It's unbelievable that a house like this would sit vacant for that long or that Mom would not have known.

I look back up to the house again. My opinion from the middle of the night hasn't changed. There is something off about this house, something I can't put my finger on. I still don't see any cars in the driveway, and I haven't seen any movement inside the house.

Instead of going to the front door, I meander back towards the woods I just came through and around the back of the house, looking around to make sure I don't have any observers.

The first thing I notice in the backyard is my mom's garden, her favorite thing in the world, in ruins. The fact that the structure of the garden remains at all is shocking, but to find it overgrown with weeds and falling apart is heartbreaking. I only remember it from pictures, but I know how my mom felt about her gardens. She would have been crushed to see this.

Whoever moved in here hadn't taken care of a thing in the backyard. It's almost like the front is only maintained to keep up appearances, and the back is left forgotten.

I walk over to the window closest to me and peek inside. My eyes are met with complete darkness. It's too dark, as though there is something blocking the window, preventing anyone from seeing in or out.

I move to the next window and find the same black nothingness.

I take a deep breath and sit down on the grass, out of view from any doors or windows in the back. I have to think this one through. With the windows blocked, I can't know if there is anyone inside. If there are people in there, could they see me snooping even though I can't see them?

It doesn't matter. Maybe I am having one of those gut feelings, but I know I have to get in there. Hearing that no one lives here, true or not, gives me the courage to execute my breaking-and-entering plan. Maybe I can find some clue in there, some remnant of the past if no one else has ever lived here. I simply need to figure out how to get in without attracting attention from nearby neighbors.

Suddenly, a vague memory of a separate part of the house resurfaces. I used to always walk into a long hallway near the kitchen. I would get in trouble all the time because the door leading back into the house from the hallway would latch on its own and I would get stuck there until Mom found me. That hallway led to the laundry room which had a door to the outside. I was sitting only a few feet from that door now. If that area is as separate from the rest of the house as I remember, there won't necessarily be anyone waiting there.

If there were even people inside at all, I remind myself, trying to give myself another confidence boost.

Before going inside, I send Aiden another message. He still hasn't responded, but I want someone to know where I am just in case. Worst case, he can call the police down here if he doesn't hear from me again.

Hey. I'm back at the house, and all is quiet so far. I'm going in. Just wanted you to know. Let me know if you uncover any other information!

I wait a minute to see if I get a response but the phone doesn't buzz.

I stand up, keep my body low as I head toward the door.

I find the door locked, but the lock is so rusty it takes almost nothing to pick it. The last thing I want to do is make any noise, but it's surprisingly easy to get inside. I shake my head, noticing the blackout paper on the window as I sidle down the long hallway.

Looking around the laundry room and down the hallway, I see dust everywhere. The washer and dryer look 30 years old, and the once-white wooden shelves are rotting out and completely bare. The rest of the cramped room looks empty. If I remember correctly, we used to have pictures lining either side of the otherwise plain hallway. Now, there were watermarks ruining the wallpaper I distinctly remember because of how awful it was.

The house truly feels abandoned. My heart is breaking, but I still can't figure out why I care. For vague memories of a childhood that doesn't feel real in this broken home? For knowing exactly how Mom would feel if she were here to see this? Whatever the reason, it doesn't matter. I can't care about any of that now.

I get to the door that I remember always getting stuck but find it wide open. A quiet sigh of relief escapes me. I can see straight through to the kitchen and catch a glimpse of old appliances, also covered in dust, and nothing on the countertops. I wait by the edge of the door so I can listen for footsteps, talking, deep breathing, anything.

After a few minutes of nothing, I step into the kitchen. A wave of nostalgia overcomes my senses as I somehow recognize our old kitchen table sitting on tile floors that look straight out of the 1970s. Shag carpet covers the adjacent room, which, judging by the stale orange couches, recliner, and old box tv, is the living room. There is even a little chest in the corner that looks like it might've held toys or dolls for a child. For me.

The house looks like it's been frozen in time since the day we moved out.

Another wave of sadness threatens to take over as I consider the possibility that the woman might've been right, that no one has lived here since Mom moved us all to the west coast of Florida.

I start feeling sorry for Mom but snap out of it quickly as I remind myself why I'm here. She sold the house and moved on. Or maybe she didn't, based on the fact that it appears as though no one else has occupied the space since. Maybe that was her secret. Dad had set her up financially, so she could keep this place as long as she wanted.

But I've seen the documents proving she sold the house back in 2004.

I continue walking through the rest of the house and poke my head into what must've been my old bedroom. It's filled with books, stuffed animals, and a bed shaped to resemble a princess castle.

The crib and rocking chair in the next room signal that it was most likely Abby's room.

I pass two doors next that look small enough to be closets, but one turns out to be a small bathroom. There is one more door a little further down the hallway which I assume should be the master bedroom.

It doesn't seem like anyone is in the house with me, and toys aren't going to give me any clues. I'm not quite ready to see the bedroom of the parents I never really had, so I start back toward the front of the house.

When I open the next door that I come across, I instantly sense the room grow cold, and my blood turns to ice. I find myself inside the garage and staring directly at a grey minivan.

I turn back into the house, walking back toward that last bedroom door with a sense of urgency now, trying not to throw up what little I have in my stomach.

"Abby?" I hear my voice, halfway between a whisper and a shout.

Nothing.

I shove that last door open, not caring who I find on the other side, but there is no one in the bedroom. The door to the master bathroom is closed, though.

"Abby?" I say, louder this time. The door is locked, but as I start picking it up, I hear a frantic humming noise. After a minute, I manage to throw the door open and find...

"Abby?!"

The humming, which had been coming from Abby, grows even more frantic as she jumps up and down. Her hands and ankles are tied together, and her mouth is taped shut.

"Abby, Abby, calm down. I'm right..." I'm in the middle of untying her mouth when I see someone sitting on the floor behind her, tears streaming down her face.

"KARA?" I practically shout.

I quickly finish untying Abby and start working on Kara. Both throw their arms around me as soon as I finish.

Abby looks as though she has been trapped in a dark room for days. She is still wearing the same clothes I saw her in at the coffee shop, and she has marks on both wrists that tell me she's been tied up most, if not all, of the time she's been missing. She has a large bruise on the side of her face that looks fresh, and she doesn't look like she has had any opportunity to shower or clean up. Her hair is knotted, and she still has last week's makeup on.

The guilt that washes over me then is so severe I almost start crying right then and there. One glance at Kara reminds me that I'll have plenty of time for that later. She doesn't look much better than Abby does, with bruises on her arms and a fresh-looking cut down her left cheek. It's hard for me to gauge how long she could have been held here for.

When was the last time I talked to her?

"Does someone want to tell me what the *hell* is going on here? Abby? Are you guys okay? Kara, how the hell are you mixed up in whatever is going on here? Were you here when I talked to you last night?" My wide range of emotions and high stress cause my words to come out different, sharper than what I intended, but I know they both understand.

Kara nods her head, keeping her eyes on the floor as Abby starts to explain.

"Listen, we don't have a lot of time. He will be back. This has everything to do with what I was trying to tell you at the coffee shop. I didn't know my stupid secret would lead to all of this, but it's all because of that secret. I can explain everything as soon as we get far, far away from this place. Did you drive here?"

"Yes, my car is right on the other side of those trees on the side of the house. Who is 'he'?"

"I…"

Abby is interrupted by a deep male voice I don't recognize, but I know I will never forget.

"Welcome home, Rachel."

CHAPTER 13 – FEBRUARY 2024

EVELYN

I sit in my jail cell of a hospital bed watching whatever game show happens to be on TV. Somebody is guessing a letter or the answer to a question in order to win some money, and it all just bores me.

This is the part I hate about being in a hospital. While it's not the first time in my nearly 47 years that I've been in a hospital bed, this certainly has been the longest. I got my diagnosis, finally, two days ago. My girls were with me then, of course. Neither of them are here now. They both still have lives of their own to live, and they have been with me constantly for the past week or so. I don't think I'll hear from Abby again today whether she is busy or not, but the selfish part of me hoped that Rachel might at least make an appearance. Maybe she will later.

Now, I only feel like I'm wasting precious minutes. The minutes matter when you hear you only have months left. Every minute becomes more valuable.

I made peace with my fate almost as soon as I heard my diagnosis. In some ways, I feel I deserve this. It's the universe's way of correcting all of my wrongdoings.

Of course, that thought doesn't make sitting here, alone and left to dwell, any easier.

I look back up at the TV I still don't care about. I turn instead to look at the book I just started reading on my bedside table. I won't have much time to read outside of the hospital, and it's hard to get into a book you know you'll never finish. Nothing interests me at the moment, which makes being stuck here so much worse.

I would kill to be able to sit with this news alone in my garden.

I let out a loud sigh as a nurse walks in to check on me. I wave her off, telling her the only thing I need is a doctor to discharge me. She smiles at me and lets me know that someone will be in soon, like reading from a script.

Someone does come in very soon after that, but it isn't my doctor. I watch this man, tall and stocky, the hood of his black sweatshirt lifted, enter my room. I wonder if he's in the wrong spot, in the wrong room, or perhaps on the wrong floor.

As his hood comes down, though, I feel my heart stop momentarily. I instantly see that he is exactly where he intends to be.

I am staring into the eyes of a ghost.

"I heard you were dying." I hear the words as though I'm underwater. Someone is screaming at me, but the words are muffled. Still, I pick up on the smug amusement in his tone.

"Scott?" The quake in my voice betrays the composure I'm desperately trying to maintain. "You're dead."

"You made a mistake," he sneers.

"How are you here? How are you alive?" I question, ignoring his accusation.

"You told Abigail what we did."

"She deserves to know the truth. Just like I do right now." I take a deep breath before continuing. "How. Are. You. Alive?" I emphasize every word, my composure returning.

"I have a wife, did you know? Kids, a family. I can't risk what I have, can't risk my life with them, all because you can't keep a secret."

I cannot believe what I am hearing. Or seeing, for that matter. I don't think I'm even fully aware of what's happening. Am I dreaming? Hallucinating? What meds do the doctors have me on here?

"You… you left us?" The realization is cutting deep – I can't keep the hurt from my voice, though he doesn't deserve to know anything about how I feel right now. I start breathing so fast that I think I might pass out.

"I left you so that you could have a better life. I was *protecting* you, just like I'm protecting my family right now. I could not look at Abigail without the guilt overwhelming me, without the fear of being caught rattling around in my mind. I couldn't handle those consequences. That's the truth if you want to hear it. And all you ever wanted was to be a mom. You were so good at it, too, once you stopped feeling so goddamn sorry for yourself." I flinch, and he pauses, shaking his head as he reflects on moments of the past. "You put me in a bad position, and I couldn't handle it. That's on me. But I *did* protect you. I could only set you and the girls up the way I did if I was no longer living. I was only trying to protect you."

I laugh, but there is no humor in the sound. I stare daggers in his direction as I spit out my next words. "Get off your high horse, Scott. Protect us? You *left* us. You left me to handle everything – my grief, living with what we did alone, raising those girls alone. You don't know the first thing about protecting anyone other than yourself. You're doing the same thing now. Your wife and kids will probably be better off without you if that's what all this comes down to. You are no different now than you were then. You're still nothing more than a disgusting coward."

Scott flinches but proceeds. "Well, we all make mistakes, don't we?" he shrugs. "But I'm going to learn from mine. This time I will do *anything* to keep my family from falling apart. That makes me determined. Not a coward. And you don't want to piss off someone as determined as I am." He spits his last words at me like venom, and the threat in his words is clear. He will do anything to keep Abby and I from speaking about this again.

"I am well aware of the sins I have committed, of my part in our downfall. I had no choice but to stay, especially after you left. I gave everything I have to those girls, and I'm done fighting what I did now. Do and say your worst to me. As you so kindly pointed out, I *am* dying. I know that I deserve everything I'm getting."

"Oh, I'm not worried about you. You won't talk. Not when you would implicate yourself and risk losing your last few months with your daughters."

"Then…"

"Abigail has so much life left to live. You would certainly care if she suddenly and tragically loses her ability to share our little secret with anyone else."

"You would harm your own daughter?" I still can't believe what I'm hearing. The shock hits like a slap in the face and every instinct I have tells me to run, tells me to warn Abby.

"She's not my daughter," he reminds me, bitterly. "She's a problem I never should've created."

"But you were protecting me," I fire back with so much acid in my tone, I could've melted metal. I do not hold back on the sarcasm and the disgust I'm feeling.

He looks me over then, as though weighing what he will say next. With a straight face and no emotion at all, he explains, "If Abigail tells anyone anything, I will kill her. If she tells Rachel, I will kill them both. If you say a word about this, about our conversation today or the things we did so long ago, I will make sure you get to bury your daughters and spend the rest of your short, miserable life alone."

He means every single word he says, and I feel my blood run cold. "What happened to you?"

He ignores my question as he walks back towards the door. I begin to wonder how no one has heard us talking. No one has come in despite our volume, despite the tension that I guarantee can be felt throughout the whole wing of this hospital.

Scott resolves that question and so many others when he stops suddenly in the doorway and looks me dead in the eyes. "In case you're wondering, I have eyes and ears in places you would never guess. Do not tell a soul, or I promise you will regret it. Although, maybe you should tell Abigail we talked today. It's only fair that she is properly warned."

His last warning feels more like an afterthought like he's mentioning this out of the goodness of his heart and not because he's enjoying whatever game he's playing. The realization of the subtle threat in his words causes me to physically blackout from fear. He says something else on his way out the door, but I can't quite process it yet. More threats, I'm sure.

The last bit of composure I had been holding onto leaves as I watch Scott finally disappear down the hallway. The fear that overwhelms me now isn't for myself but for my girls. They were *my* girls, I realize. Not his. Neither of those girls is his, or he would never be able to say the things he said about them.

I grab my phone from the bedside table as soon as I'm able to speak. I know I need to call Abby right away, but as my fingers fumble over the buttons on my phone, Scott's final threat plays on a loop over and over again in my head. I finally register what he said as he walked out the door, and I feel my heart begin to race again. I imagine all life leaving my body right then and there.

"After you're gone, there will be no one here to protect her anymore. I will do whatever I need to in order to protect myself and this secret. Consider that a promise."

CHAPTER 14 – JUNE 2024

RACHEL

I turn around to see a man I recognize, though it takes me a second to realize why. He has the same eyes as me, though the crow's feet surrounding them prove time has passed since the last picture we took together. The soft brown hair I remember from those pictures is now sprinkled with salt and pepper, and the sun spots and wrinkles on his brow age him considerably.

I am staring at the ghost of a man who should've stopped aging 20 years ago.

And yet…

I can feel the blood draining from my face, my whole body, as I remind myself to breathe.

That seems to be happening a lot lately.

"D-dad?"

Breathe. Breathe. In and out. In and out.

"In the flesh." He bows, like he's a stage performer at the end of his final act. "So glad you could finally join us. Although I am surprised to hear you still call me that after all of the poison your mother and sister drilled into your head."

"What are you talking about?" I demand, confusion and anger taking over my expression. "How are you even alive? You've just left Mom alone all these years?"

He laughs, but there is no humor in it. "That bitch got everything she deserved for what she put *me* through. That is all I'll say about her."

I make to leap at him, to strike him, anything to release the anger threatening to boil over, but Abby holds me back. I gape at her, unable to conceal the flash of hurt that crosses my features. When I notice her eyes flashing from mine to where Scott's hand rests – on a gun holstered to his hip – I settle back down next to her, nodding my understanding.

"What is going on? Why are Kara and Abigail tied up in the bathroom of the house we grew up in, and *how are you alive.*"

"So, Victoria really didn't tell you? Interesting." Is he…amused?

"Abby," I hear my sister snap before I can register the name he just used.

"Not technically, but you knew that already." He winks at her. *Winks.*

This is all a joke to him. He finds something inherently funny about a situation the rest of us don't understand. Or, I realize quickly, *I* don't understand. All I have gathered so far is that there is a secret he thinks we all know, and he wants that secret kept in the dark.

It takes me another second, but the pieces start falling together one by one…

"Wait, Victoria? Like the missing little girl, Victoria Wright?" I exclaim.

"That's the one!" Scott confirms, animatedly pointing in my direction. His energy is unsettling, and he looks almost… proud. "You have done your research!"

"What does she have to do with…" I stop, mid-sentence, when I look over to find my sister with her eyes glued to the ground. "You're her. You're the girl who went missing all those years ago." Not a question. Aiden was onto something when he connected those dates.

I watch Abby nod in slow motion, as though she was afraid of confirming her secret. Afraid that the confirmation would somehow place the blame for this on her shoulders. Afraid it would mean losing me forever. She won't even look me in the eye.

It sort of fit everything that I had found out, though. That little girl was kidnapped around the same time my sister's record of death showed her as deceased. Aiden even pointed out the proximity. If the situation is to be believed, both incidents happened near here. Scott's suicide note, what he said about not living with the guilt, the blanket I found in the closet of Abby's old room. My mind refuses to complete the picture all of these details make, though. There is too much information coming in to process it all at once.

"How long have you known?" I try to keep my voice light, but I'm sure I'm doing a terrible job.

"Just since that day in the hospital. Mom told me everything."

I turn to Scott. "The suicide note – you kidnapped her. Why? What happened to Abigail?"

"I knew you'd find it!! That's how you figured it out! Where we were!" I can feel the excitement out of place, radiating off her. I try to send her a warning glance, to scold her for the outburst, but Scott's stony glare does that first. She backs down as though retreating into a shell.

"If we're splitting hairs here, Scott Stephens kidnapped Victoria Wright. I go by Shane Walker these days." He reaches out a hand as though introducing himself at a cocktail party.

All three of us stare at the outstretched hand in disgust until he puts it down. "Alright, not in the mood for jokes this morning."

I'm dumbfounded and growing increasingly impatient for answers. "Wh-why?" I stutter through the simple question I'm asking, even though I know there is no explanation that could ever make me understand.

"Because the mother you love and admire so much killed your baby sister. Drowned her in this very bathtub one night when I was held up at work."

No mincing words, I see. The casual sarcasm in his voice makes my stomach turn. This man is a sociopath; I think I might be sick.

"No." I shake my head vigorously, denying everything I'm hearing. No, no, no. He is lying. He has to be. I look up to Abby for support but find her eyes glued to the ground once again. "Abby?" I ask, my voice breaking, desperate.

"She was sick, Rach. Really sick, and all this asshole ever did was work. And don't let him fool you. The last two hours of his "late night at work" that night were spent at a bar. Just like every night. She didn't realize it at the time, because it wasn't really talked about, but she had postpartum depression, and she was all alone. She never asked for this, for me, for a "replacement." When Scott showed up with a baby who looked basically the same as her Abigail, she just wasn't in the right headspace to turn him away. I was hurt that night. She helped me get better."

I watch Abby subconsciously rub her arm over her tattoo where her long scar is now covered before continuing.

"This asshole put all kinds of thoughts in her head about it, had her thinking he was dad of the year or something for 'protecting her.' By the time she was getting the help she needed, she and Scott were in it too deep. Besides, she was afraid he would try to shut her up if she ever tried to say anything, and I think this" she motions around us "is proof of that. When Scott died, she didn't want that to be in vain, and she had grown to love me as her own. For whatever reason, my real family had stopped looking for me within a few days of me going missing. She said he intentionally picked the family he did because they weren't good people. They had it coming. I'm not sure I buy anything he tries to sell, but she didn't feel like she had a choice at the time."

"She's right," I hear Scott chime in, as if from a distance. My mind is processing everything Abby just told me, though not very well. "Evelyn never asked me to do what I did. I did it to protect our family. To protect my family. Just like I'm doing now."

"You're protecting us by...kidnapping us?"

"Oh, no. Please don't be confused. No, I don't care about the three of you. I only care about the threat you now represent to my family. My way of life. I have a beautiful wife, a girl, and a boy who are my world, and I cannot have that ruined by your lack of discretion." He looks directly at me then. "I do apologize, Rachel. I was certain you knew more than you should. I was wrong, and now I've got you stuck in the middle of all this mess."

Somehow, his apology doesn't seem sincere.

"Abby and I won't say anything. We promise. And Kara has nothing to do with this."

"I'm aware. I only took her to find out how much you knew. I knew you didn't know anything serious once I went through your phone – sorry about the robbery situation, by the way. A bit dramatic, if you ask me – but then you started poking your head around, worrying about your "missing sister" who had been gone for two days. You are aware that she had just been gone for months without a word, correct? Anyway, you were sent warnings to leave all of this alone, and you didn't listen. Now we're here."

"How..."

I'm interrupted again by Scott's raised hand, palm facing me like a human stop sign. "You would be surprised how easy it is to get access to the number of your little prepaid phone when you're able to properly threaten the idiot behind the cash register of the convenience store you stop at."

"But how..." Again, I'm interrupted but not by Scott this time. Another man with a short, lean frame and white hair walks up to

Scott, standing just outside the doorway of the bathroom that Scott was still blocking.

The man begins whispering something in Scott's ear, and I catch a glimpse of his facial features. The glasses, the wrinkles that make him look at least 10 years older than he is, the mole on the left side of his nose. No way...

"Glenn?" I start. The shock and hurt are evident in my voice.

This man, who had looked out for us when we were kids, spent holidays with us, befriended Evelyn, comforted me when I was all alone just *days* ago, is somehow mixed up with this despicable excuse for my father.

Glenn's eyes only flash to me briefly before he averts his gaze. He seems to take a page from Abby's book and glues his eyes to the floor. He begins to walk away, but Scott grabs his arm and pulls him directly in front of him, blocking his exit from the small bathroom along with the rest of us.

It's starting to get crowded in here.

"Rachel, Victoria, please let me introduce you to my little watchdog." A show host playing his part once again, he pats Glenn on the back with a laugh as he continues, "Oh, my. Do you all know each other?" he asks in mock surprise.

"Glenn, how could you? What would Betty say?" It's Abby who speaks first, acid in her voice. I'm still at a loss for words. Every time my brain starts processing the new information I get, a new bombshell is dropped right at my feet.

"Girls, you know how much I care for you both," he pleads, genuine sorrow in his eyes.

"Do you?" I snap. I don't care how sorry he is now. It's too late for sorry.

"Of course. You both were like the daughters Betty and I never had. You have to understand. I was only ever supposed to keep tabs, to make sure Evelyn never spoke of the past, what she and Sco… Shane, sorry," he shoots an apologetic glance toward the other man, "had done." The approval he seeks from Scott, as though making sure he is saying the right things, makes me thankful I haven't had anything to eat in practically 24 hours. It might have ended up on the floor right then and there.

"Glenn, don't be modest. Don't forget to tell them about all the money you made off the deal!"

I have never looked at someone with as much disgust as I was now aiming in Glenn's direction. "So, it's your fault we're all in this mess."

"No, actually. It's your mother's fault," Scott chimes in.

I can tell Abby is starting to get pissed. She steps in front of me then, standing inches from Glenn. Close enough that they should be able to feel each other breathing.

"Don't you," she looks back and forth between the two men, "either of you, say a single word about our mother."

"She's not your mother." Scott spat the words at her with so much venom, like a snake striking for the kill.

I watch what happens next as though in slow motion. I might've been able to stop it, but my body just doesn't move. It hits me then why Scott positioned Glenn in front of him.

Abby's swing lands right in the center of Scott's jaw, but not as hard as it would've if she hadn't had to reach around Glenn to land it. Still, I can already tell he is going to have a nasty bruise tomorrow.

I watch Scott recover and spit blood on the floor, mostly unfazed and very little blood, but Abby had gotten her point across. Glenn reacts quickly trying hard to push Abby back towards the bathtub we are all still standing around. Kara is still standing off to the side, not making much noise, and Abby is thrown into her. After that, she stops fighting and sits back down on the edge of the large tub.

"Nothing but a bunch of ungrateful brats. You don't even know who you're defending, or whose reputation you're trying to preserve. What she did is unforgivable. Yet, she has you thinking I'm the bad guy."

"We don't know a single thing about you. She never said a word about you, good or bad, but I know she was my mother in all the ways that count." Abby starts out soft before finding her voice again. "I know that you abandoned her. You abandoned all of us. You've been god-knows-where for the past twenty years and you're back now only to save yourself. Doing it under the pretense of being a family man doesn't make you a hero. You only care about yourself. She spent our whole lives trying to make her mental and physical sacrifice worth it, trying to make up for what she had done, all while trying to forgive herself for a tragedy that you only wanted to cover up. She needed a husband, a friend, a shoulder. And all you could think about was your twisted idea of what it means to be a protector. Just like you're doing now."

Scott looks as though he is absorbing everything she is saying, processing it, and thinking about how to respond. I can only look at Abby in awe. After everything she has been through, she was defending Mom. Maybe this means there is hope for us, too? Maybe she can forgive me, too?

"You girls don't have a clue. What it comes down to is that she opened her mouth when she shouldn't have, and she put you in danger. But she knew that, too. Isn't that why she told you to run and not come back until the dust settled, Victoria?"

Abby doesn't answer.

To everyone's surprise, Kara speaks up, her voice broken but her confidence growing with every word. "Clearly, I don't know you, dude. But I know Evelyn, and I love these girls. I would do anything for them. We are more of a family than anything you will ever have. Despite all her secrets, Evelyn raised a family all by herself, and she was cherished and loved by everyone she met.

You will never know love or family like what they had, what they will always have, no matter what venom you feel the need to spit today. You're nothing more than a coward."

On Kara's final word, Scott looks ready to do something drastic, loathing in his eyes, but instead, he snarls and says, "I really just wanted to talk, ladies. That's all. Glenn, deal with them." He motions for Glenn to tie us back up.

All three of us stand to fight Glenn off, but he is quicker. He is closest to Kara, so he turns to push her into the shower door first. He doesn't push hard, but Kara loses her balance and falls, hitting her head on the corner of the bathtub.

"Kara!" I scream, but Glenn is coming right at me now.

"Glenn, come on. You don't want to do this," I plead.

"I don't have a choice, Rach. I don't want to hurt you. Please. Just help me make this easy for both of us."

I only hesitate for a second, considering my next move, before my knee collides with his groin, and he doubles over in pain. Abby, who was standing behind Glenn, kicks him in the stomach for good measure while he's still bent over on the floor.

"I guess I'll get my hands dirty now," Scott grumbles to himself. "Shut up with your whining, would you? You, useless old man," he barks at Glenn, who is still doubled over on the floor, choking on air. He doesn't show any signs of being able to get up, which only seems to infuriate Scott more.

Abby and I look at each other, knowing neither of us is going to go down without a fight. I throw myself at Scott's knees, trying to take him off his feet right away. He steps out of the way before I can make contact, and I land hard on my stomach. As he turns around to look at where I landed, Abby jumps toward his back, fully intending to jump on top of his shoulders and get as many punches in as she can.

She closes the distance swiftly but only gets close enough to deliver a punch to the center of his spine. He stumbles, the impact throwing him off balance, and he staggers backward right toward me. From my position on the ground, I am at the perfect angle to kick him hard in the back of his knees. He collapses with a grunt, hitting the floor with a heavy thud. Adrenaline surges through me as I scramble to my feet, ready for whatever comes next.

The whole fight is starting to feel too easy when Scott yells, "Alright, that's enough!" His voice is laced with anger, and I can see now that this won't be an easy fight after all. He's been toying with us, just playing a game of cat and mouse, letting us believe we had a chance before landing his final blow.

Scott stands, and with smooth, practiced motion, pulls the gun from his hip – the same gun he had been resting his hand against earlier. The glint of metal catches my eye and my pulse quickens. This is no longer a game; the stakes have just skyrocketed.

"The only reason I kept the three of you alive this long was to find out how much that one knew." He jabs a finger in my direction. "None of you idiots seem to have told anyone else, so the secrets die with you. You've had your fun now, but you all know too much. This is how it has to end."

Abby spits, *actually spits*, in his face.

"Alright, you've made my next decision easy. The worst thing I ever did was take you. I should've let Evelyn rot in this bathroom with nothing but her guilt and our dead baby. It would've saved us all a lot of trouble. You go first."

He cocks the gun and points it directly at Abby's face. We both freeze, our breaths caught in our throats. The room seems to shrink around us, the air thick with tension. Every second stretches, an eternity passing as we stare down the barrel of the gun, our minds racing for a way out.

"I wouldn't do that if I were you."

That voice. I recognize that voice…

I force myself to stay calm, the gun still a very real threat in Scott's hand. Inside, though, I'm screaming with joy. It is taking everything in me not to run to the voice that Scott is now turning toward.

He came! He actually came!

I glance at Abby, hoping to share my relief, but her face is a mask of confusion. She doesn't realize what's happening yet.

Scott whips around to confront the unexpected stranger. "Who the hell are you?"

Gun in one hand and badge in another, the man smiles and introduces himself. "Aiden Cooper. Manatee County Sherriff's office. You're in a lot of trouble."

"You have no jurisdiction here," Scott snaps and points his gun at Aiden instead of Abby. "No one thought to mention we might have more guests joining us?" He directs this ire at Glenn, not expecting an answer. Glenn only whimpers.

"No, but I brought it back up." Aiden moves to reveal cops from the Miami Dade police force standing behind him, guns all aimed toward Scott. "It may be in your best interest to come with me and not cause any further trouble."

Scott lowers his gun, and I breathe a sigh of relief. But then, in a split second, he raises it again, this time aiming at Aiden. Time seems to slow as I see his finger tighten on the trigger.

"No!" I scream, but the sound is drowned out by the deafening crack of a gunshot.

I feel Abby catch me as I collapse to the floor, my vision swimming. The world around me blurs, but through the haze, I see her worried face hovering above mine. Just as my consciousness slips away, I hear Abby's frantic voice calling my name, her grip tightening. Perhaps it's the guilt I feel for bringing him into this mess, or perhaps my feelings run deeper than that now. More than likely, it is a combination of both feelings that conjure up his face in my mind.

Aiden is the last thing I think about before the darkness consumes me.

When my eyes flutter open, I find myself staring at a clear blue sky. I'm lying on my back but not on the hard, tile floor of the bathroom I last remember being in. I start feeling around me only to catch blades of grass in my fingers.

Immediately, panic sets in. How did I get outside? Where are Kara and Abby? Is Aiden alive?

I try to sit up, and feel two strong, firm hands press my shoulders back to the ground. The touch isn't forceful, but I can tell the hands don't belong to my sister or my best friend.

I try to sit up again, a little more aggressively this time; I'll be damned if anyone tries to keep me from getting up, from getting to Abby, when I have no idea what's going on.

"Hey, hey," I hear a gentle voice trying to calm me. "Abby and Kara are fine. You passed out, and you need to take it easy for a few minutes."

Aiden's face comes into view as he explains, and I feel as though I might faint again.

"Aiden? You're okay? I heard a gunshot."

Everyone is fine. I can stop panicking.

"Yeah. Unfortunately, I had to stop Scott. He was ready to take us all out had he been given the chance." He sees the shock in my face and quickly adds, "He's alive. I just got him in the leg, knocked the gun away. To stop him, not to kill him. We have him detained in the back of a police car. He has way too much to answer for."

"Abby and Kara?"

"Kara needs to go to the hospital. She hit her head pretty hard on that bathtub. She's awake, but there's a cut on her head, and she may have a concussion. Abby is getting checked out, too, but she refuses to go anywhere until you're awake." He laughs to himself, amused by something I don't understand, as he waves to someone else in the distance.

The next thing I know, he's handing me a water bottle and helping me into a sitting position. "How are you feeling? I was worried about you. What if I hadn't gotten here in time?"

"I'm fine. I just want to see Abigail." I sound much more patient than I feel. I think he's trying to scold me, but it's not working for him, and I don't really want to hear it right now anyway. I appreciate his concern, but my only concern at the moment is my sister.

"Okay, just take a couple of sips of water first. I want to make sure you aren't feeling lightheaded or dizzy before you get moving."

I take two quick sips of water and stand up, Aiden's arm on my back the whole way.

"How did you find us, anyway?"

"You told me you were going to the house you grew up in. It wasn't hard to find the address once I looked into those old cases and found information on your dad's apparent suicide. We're going to confirm this, but it looks as though your Mom sold the house, unknowingly, to someone who had a close connection with Scott in the past. They sold the house, almost immediately, to someone named Shane Walker."

"That's Scott."

"Who is Scott?"

"Shane Walker. Scott told us he goes by Shane Walker now." I pause for a second before asking, "How did you know to bring back up? We didn't even know if anyone was in the house."

"I didn't. But unlike you," he shoots me a disapproving look, "I wasn't taking any chances. I called in a favor from someone I used to work with, explained the situation, and these guys all met me here. Good thing, too."

I can only nod. "Can I see my sister now?"

"Of course! As long as you feel steady on your feet."

I motion up and down my entire body, as though that proves anything, before saying, "All good!" I can see the ambulance at the end of the driveway and begin walking toward it before hesitating.

I don't know what makes me decide to do it, but I walk back over to Aiden and throw my arms around him, hoping the hug will be well received and not a complete overstep. "Thank you so much for everything," I whisper into his shoulder. For less than a second, I can tell he's surprised by my sudden show of affection, but he recovers quickly and wraps his arms around my waist, lightly kissing the side of my head.

I pull back, staring at his lips for a second too long, lips that I suddenly want to kiss, before shaking my head and running to the ambulance, leaving Aiden there to watch me walk away.

CHAPTER 15 – JUNE 2024

RACHEL

I stick my head into the back of the ambulance and find Kara strapped to a stretcher, hooked up to an IV. Abigail is sitting on the small bench next to Kara with her head in her hands.

She must have seen me approaching out of the corner of her eye, because, without lifting her head, I hear her say, "She's okay. She was awake for a bit. Just sleeping now." She still doesn't look up at me.

"Good." I can't think of anything else to say.

"I asked them to wait until you could see her, see that she was okay. You passed out when your boyfriend shot Scott. He said he could take care of you, so I didn't have to leave Kara alone."

My face flushes instantly. "He's not my boyfriend!"

She looks up at me then with a giant grin on her face, rolling her eyes. "Oh, please! Don't act like I don't know all your tells. Your face is bright red!"

"Okay, okay. I will admit, begrudgingly I might add, that I do find him incredibly attractive. But that's all. I just met him this week! He's been helping me find you, that's all."

"Yeah, well he might have an ulterior motive," she jokes.

"He's working." I brush her off with a bad excuse and an eye roll of my own.

She starts to climb out of the ambulance, trying her best to not bump into Kara. "Yeah, he's four hours outside of his jurisdiction when he could've just made a phone call, but he's totally 'working' right now." Her fingers form quote marks as I try to help her down. "When you guys get married, I expect a massive thank-you gift."

I crack up knowing I somehow have the same exact Abby back, the Abby from before mom's diagnosis with her sarcastic comments and quick judgements. Like the past four months never happened, even though she still seems to have trouble looking me in the eye.

When she has two feet firmly planted on the ground, Abby throws her arms around my neck in a hug so tight I couldn't escape it even if I wanted to.

"Rach, I am so, so, so sorry for everything. I thought I was doing the right thing. I thought I was keeping you safe, and then I put you in danger anyway by coming back. Please promise you'll let me explain everything before you decide to hate me."

My words come out muffled as I'm practically stuck in a headlock. "Abby, how could I hate you? You're my sister. We need to talk everything out, but none of this is your fault."

She's shaking now. "You heard him in there. He wasn't lying, you know? I really am this other person, Victoria Wright."

I pull back so I can look her in the eye when I reassure her. "Hey, whatever this is, whoever you are, you're my sister. You're the Abby that I know and love with all my heart. This doesn't change that. We'll figure this out together. Just breathe."

As Abby nods, her hands still clutching mine, a young EMT walks up behind her and startles us both.

"You ladies doing okay? We're going to get your friend here over to Kendall." Our blank expressions prompt her to add, "The hospital."

I nod and let her know that Abby and I can meet them over there. As we begin walking toward my car, I can't stop myself from taking a quick glance around, and I struggle to mask my disappointment when I don't find what I'm looking for.

"Don't worry. He thinks you're hot, too." Abby playfully jabs me in the arm with her elbow.

I shove her, laughing, but do my best to keep my eyes from wandering the entire rest of the walk back to the car. It's much easier to keep my footing in the daylight, but the same can't be said for Abby.

"I can't believe you're making me walk through the woods. Can't you just pick me up over here?"

"You whine so much!" I laugh. "I told you I'd get you hiking one of these days. This was actually all an elaborate plan to force you into nature for a grand total of 5 minutes. You're doing great so far!"

"I did just barely survive a kidnapping, you know? A little sympathy would be appreciated."

"Yes, and you're welcome for saving your life!"

We joke the whole way back to the car which seems to make the walk a little easier on Abby and takes the edge off for both of us.

As we drive to the hospital, Abby begins filling me in on everything.

Mom had told her, briefly, everything that happened 20 years ago – how she struggled with postpartum depression, how she had accidentally killed her daughter, Abigail, and what Scott had done to "fix it," although one could argue that he never actually fixed anything.

"Mom and I, we were almost never alone. You and I were both with her so much. I think she saw an opportunity when she sent you to get lunch. Not her best timing, I will admit, but she didn't want to die leaving me in the dark, and she had just gotten a death sentence. I think part of her panicked a little. She asked me to talk more and, I'm not proud of this, but I was so pissed, I just left. Imagine finding out your whole life is a lie in a 20-minute conversation.

"I went back the next morning after cooling off, and that's when she told me everything. It was a lot for me, you know? Your mom isn't really your mom? Your best friend in the whole world, your sister, shouldn't even be in your life. Your dad, who died in a car accident 20 years ago actually killed himself? Mom had really been all alone this whole time, and I could only think about what this all meant for me. I just needed time to process."

"Abby, it's been *months*. I understand needing time, but I've been alone, too. I buried Mom *alone*." I try to keep the hurt out of my voice, but I'm not sure I succeed.

"I know. And I know you will never be able to forgive me for that, but there's more." She takes a deep breath before continuing. "I don't know how Glenn found out, or maybe Scott has minions in more places than we realized, but Scott came to the hospital the day after she explained everything to me. He threatened her, threatened us. In his mind, it was bad enough that she had told me. If you ever found out, he threatened to make her bury her own daughters."

I can hear Abby's breathing deepen. She's holding back tears as she continues.

"Rach, I've never heard her so scared in my life. I was going to take a few days to process on my own, and then maybe go back and find you, talk to Mom more. I still have so many questions for her. She felt like me leaving, staying away for a while, was a deserving punishment for her part in everything, but she also believed it would keep both of us safe. I argued for a while, but she was terrified, and not budging. It seemed like my only option. I know that means we both lied to you, and I am sorry for that, but that was the reason."

We are both silent for a few moments before Abby continues again.

"He hurt me that night, you know? That's how I got this scar." She points to the spot on her arm now almost covered by the tattoo. "Mom said it was like being on autopilot, jumping right into mom-mode. She wasn't sad in that moment because she had to switch gears mentally and help me. He was a drunk. And, Mom never explicitly stated it, but I don't think he was a very nice drunk. I just think she knew what he was capable of back then, and who knows how much worse he's gotten since. I guess we do now. That man is unhinged."

"That's the understatement of the century," I agree.

"She just wanted to keep you safe. I just wanted to keep you safe."

It only takes a few minutes to reach the hospital. I pull into a parking spot facing an entrance marked EMERGENCY.

I turn the car off but make no move to get out of the car. I'm staring at the dash of the car for about a minute when a soft, hesitant voice asked, "Rach?"

"I understand." I begin moving my head up and down, as though trying to convince myself that I do. "Selfishly, I needed you, and you weren't here. But I think that you also needed me, and you were alone, too. I think, for the past 10 minutes, I've just been trying to understand why you felt like you couldn't tell me, that the three of us couldn't have figured this out together. Now I look at what just happened, and I realize you had an impossible choice. But it's all out in the open now. We're going to need each other now more than ever. I promise I'm not going to leave you alone through all of this again. We can attend every necessary therapy session together if that's what's needed."

Abby laughs out loud, the most carefree sound I have heard in months, and it is contagious. "We're going to need plenty of those, I think." She jokes through fits of laughter.

After the laughter dies down, Abby grows quiet again. "I did come back to tell you everything. I wanted to go to the funeral. Of course, I wanted to go to the funeral. I saw Scott's men loitering by the trees that lined the far parking lot. I didn't want to risk it, not on that day. I couldn't ruin that day, too. I thought I'd be safe coming to your apartment after, but either I was tailed, or you were already being watched." Her voice was shaking again.

"Hey, it's okay." I grab her hand. "I'm sorry that I didn't give you that time when you needed me. Despite everything that has happened, it's better that you don't have to hide anymore. None of this is your fault, okay? The only thing we absolutely need to discuss for now is the haircut and that tattoo," I joke, changing the topic to a lighter one.

"Yeah, yeah. All in good time." She shoves my arm and then leans across the center console to wrap me in an awkward hug. "I love you, Rach."

"Love you, too! Now, come on. Let's go find Kara."

When we get inside and find where Kara is waiting, she is awake and with a police officer. Abby freezes for an instant and then relaxes immediately. It seems like a strange reaction—of course, we all will be questioned at some point.

We wait in the hallway until they finish. When the officer passes us on her way out, she nods at Abby and pauses in front of me.

"I'm Officer Huntingdon." She sticks her hand out as she greets us. "We'll need to question you at some point, but I know it's been a long day. Go see your friend, and make sure you stop by the station before you head home, okay?"

"Yes, ma'am. Thank you." I shake her outstretched hand, and she turns to leave.

When the officer is out of earshot, I turn to Abby. "Is that normal? Shouldn't I be questioned immediately?"

She winks again— *what is with the winking*—and says, "It helps to have friends in high places, I guess. Or boyfriends."

"Oh, you're ridiculous!"

"Would you girls stop bickering and get in here?" Kara sounds exasperated. "Nothing ever changes with you two." I can practically hear her eye roll.

We walk over to Kara, and both of us wrap her in a hug.

"Alright, you two. Does someone want to tell me what the heck is going on?" She echoes my thoughts from earlier but in a lighthearted way.

I speak first. "Well, depending on how much you guys talked while being held hostage, I might not know much more than you do."

Abby starts by explaining everything that she hasn't told Kara yet. They had some time to talk about what was going on, but not enough for Kara to fully understand why Abby had left, why they were taken, and who that man was.

"Well, you can thank Abby here for thinking about that fake suicide note you guys both seemed to know about. I guess having very little information about your childhood makes word associations easier?" Kara asks playfully.

"Maybe, but I never would've even known about those text messages if it wasn't for Kara," Abby says. "I had no idea you were getting threats via burner phone."

"Yeah, how did you guys even get that phone?" I ask.

"I got the phone off some minion when he brought us in dinner. I got very lucky because he didn't notice, and he left the room for a few minutes before coming back for the trays. I gave it back to him, and he was pissed. You should've seen the look on his face. Of course, I found that hilarious, and that's how I got this." She points to the big cut I noticed on her face earlier. "I'm sorry for the code, too. I figure if I outright gave you a location, they would be more prepared for you to show up right away. This way, they were just as confused by the message as you probably were, but I hoped you had the means necessary to figure it out."

"Oh, Abby. I'm sorry. At least you know it was worth it." I console as best I can. "And you are lucky I found that note. Which reminds me, please don't press charges for your broken window."

Abby's head shoots up, but she quickly decides, or hopes, that I'm joking. "Yeah, it certainly was. I'm not sure why those idiots ever let Kara call you though."

"I think they were growing concerned because the text was sent already. Nothing they could do to take that back. But then you kept calling me. They assumed you were getting dangerously worried, and that me telling you to back off would actually get you to back off. I wasn't going to tell them they were wrong. First-time minions, I guess." Kara explains her theory, shrugging, and we all start laughing.

"I'm so sorry for putting you both in danger. I really thought I was doing the right thing." Abby apologizes again, even though she doesn't need to.

Kara explains her feelings on the unnecessary apology the same way I did— we would've been in danger either way. Not because of her, but because of that sociopath who kidnapped her in the first place.

"What are you going to do?" Kara asks.

"I'm not really sure. You didn't say anything about me being kidnapped, right?"

"Yeah, Detective Cooper got to me before any other officers did."

My eyes dart between them both, confused as to why that matters. Then I realize they're not talking about Abby being kidnapped as an adult. They're talking about Victoria being kidnapped 20 years ago.

"They're going to have to fight over jurisdiction, or whatever it's called, I think. Kara and I were both taken back home, but we were held here. Scott isn't going to talk, we hope, until he has a lawyer. That gives me some time. If they can take the case back to Bradenton, Detective Cooper said he can make sure that the information about me being Victoria Wright doesn't get out right away. I don't know if that's technically legal or not, but he said I can make the choice on whether or not I seek out my birth family. As far as anyone knows right now, Victoria Wright is still missing."

"Wow, that's very... generous of him?"

"Yeah, more perks of having a sister who's dating a detective." She gently nudges me, as though giving me props for an assist I didn't know I made.

"You're dating him?!" Kara begins to freak out. "He's gorgeous! Good for you!"

They both start giggling like we are back in middle school.

Glaring at Abby, I say to Kara, "No! No. Don't you have a concussion? You should be resting."

After I fully convinced both Kara and Abby that being attracted to someone does not equal dating them, we spent the next few hours laughing and catching up. When Kara is finally discharged, I make a quick stop at the police station to give my statement, leaving out the fact that Abby is Victoria Wright, and the three of us drive home together.

Kara stays with me for the night, just in case. She does, in fact, have a concussion, and she'll need to take it easy for a while.

Abby planned on moving to a new apartment once she realized the threat to her safety was real. She had given her single couch and TV set to Ms. Nosy Neighbor across the hall – a fact she had so graciously forgotten to mention when I first asked her about my sister. "It was months ago! I'm old," she just shrugs and mumbles something about being expected to remember every little detail when I questioned her about it a few days later.

She did still have her bed and all her clothes and wanted to sleep in her own bed for the first time in months. I can't blame her. I'm sure she still has a lot to process, think about, and ultimately decide on.

I wake up the next day to find Kara already in the kitchen making us coffee. "Shouldn't you need extra sleep?" I grumble. Stumbling into the kitchen, I take my cup of coffee from her. "I should be making coffee for you."

Kara shrugs her shoulders as she saunters over to the couch and turns the TV on.

"I don't think that's good for your head either!" I call out.

"Okay, mom!"

Kara puts on a TV show I don't recognize and falls asleep again within minutes. I grab the remote to change the channel when I hear a knock on the door. Glancing at the clock, I see it's only a quarter past eight. Abby is early.

I'm not even dressed yet, still in my too-short shorts and a tank top with no bra, definitely not suitable for answering the door. Quickly, I throw on a sweatshirt and some leggings before opening the door to let her in.

When I see who is standing in my doorway, though, my whole body tenses up. I silently thank all the stars in the sky that I decided to put on some real clothes.

Abby isn't early.

Aiden is standing there, looking as stunning as ever in faded black jeans and a light green t-shirt that makes his bright hazel eyes even more captivating. He's not in uniform today, and, for more than one reason, I hope I don't have to see him in it again for a long time.

He looks exhausted like he hasn't slept all night. It hits me that I have no idea when he left Miami. It's entirely possible that he hasn't slept at all.

"Aiden. Hi. What are you doing here?" Surprise colors my tone, but I'm not unhappy to see him. I'm completely caught off guard and looking like an absolute mess, but not unhappy.

"Hi, uh, I hope this is okay. I'm still not stalking you. I just wanted to check on you, see how you're doing?"

He is… nervous? Why is he so nervous?

"Um, yeah. Yeah, this is fine. I'm doing fine. Kara is here, sleeping. She's doing okay, too."

"Good. I'm really glad to hear it."

"Yeah, I'm glad no one was hurt any worse than they were."

He keeps shifting his weight from one foot to the other, his unease palpable. It's a little unsettling to see him so uncomfortable. As if just looking for something to say, he suddenly blurts out, "We're going to keep everything about your sister's true identity quiet for as long as we can."

"Yeah, she told me."

"It looks like that man, Scott, didn't cover his tracks so well. Almost like he felt he wouldn't get caught, so the details didn't matter. As soon as we get the case sorted out, it should be easy to pin everything on him, past and present."

"Okay, good."

"Yeah, he certainly has a lot of shady connections. Did you know he used to be a lawyer for one of the top law firms in the Miami area? I guess that's how he got all the money to set your Mom up so well, and to pay for all of his connections. I imagine the nature of the work he was doing is what connected him to the people who helped him along the way. It turns out, he had a hand in everyone's pocket, including my boss'."

"Yeah, I knew he was a lawyer," is all I can say. Then I add, "Is that why you were told to drop the case?"

"I'm pretty sure it was, yeah. That will be a huge mess for a while."

The conversation is making me uneasy. As much as I need to know the details, I'm not ready to hear them just yet— especially when I'm not even dressed and ready for the day and still awkwardly standing in my doorway.

"His family, I mean his current family, they're being told ever-"

I cut him off. "Aiden, I'm happy to see you. I'm really glad you're okay, and I can't thank you enough for everything you did for me and my family this past week. I just don't want to talk about that man anymore right now."

"Yes, of course not. Sorry! Of course. Listen, I didn't mean to bring that up. I'm just rambling." He looks flustered like talking about the case is his safety net. Easier than... easier than what?

"Okay, then what did you come here to talk about?" I ask, my voice a little softer now.

He stutters for a few seconds. "I—Well, I— Would it be- Would you be interested in—"

"Hey, guys!" A loud cheerful voice is coming toward us.

"Abby! Hi! Aiden stopped by to see how we were all doing." I offer an explanation for a question that hasn't been asked.

"Oh yeah, I'm sure he cares about how we're *all* doing." The sarcasm is palpable.

Aiden's cheeks flush as Abby pushes past us to go inside.

"She's here because we're going to go visit our mom's grave site. She never really got to say goodbye." I explain, gesturing over my shoulder.

"Oh." Understanding flashes in his eyes. "I won't bother you then. Enjoy your day with your sister!" He turns and walks away, not giving me a chance to respond.

I can't shake the feeling that I'm missing something *important* there.

Once we're back inside and the door is closed, Abby asks, "So, did I just save you from having to turn that poor boy down, or did I completely screw up an opportunity for you to actually get laid this decade?"

"What are you talking about?" I look at Abby like she has 3 heads. I grab one of the couch pillows Kara isn't currently using and throw it at her.

"That man was struggling so hard to ask you out. I couldn't tell if you were that freaking oblivious or if you just didn't want to have to turn him down, but I had to put him out of his misery."

"Abigail!" I pick the pillow up off the floor and actually hit her with it this time.

"Well, would you have said yes?"

"I don't know. Is that weird?"

"Not at all." A wicked grin spreads across her face.

"Whatever. He didn't ask me out, and he wasn't going to ask me out. Can we go now?" I ask, exasperated.

"Kara is okay here?" she asks, glancing at our still-sleeping friend.

"Yeah, she's fine now. Just needs to rest. We won't be too long."

I cover Kara with a blanket, and we leave to say our last goodbyes to our mom.

Most of our time at the cemetery is spent reminiscing about old memories, our childhood, our favorite things about Mom. We avoid discussing any of the negative – there will be plenty of time for that later.

The day is bright and sunny, a complete contrast to our emotions and the events of the past week. This time, though, it feels more like a sign of hope rather than the cruel joke it usually seems to be. The dirt on the ground is still fresh; it will be a while before any grass starts to grow. The small, rectangular headstone is simple, just as Mom would have wanted.

"It's perfect. I'm so sorry you had to do all this alone," Abby says, the only reference to the difficult past few months. Towards the end, Abby sits with Mom alone for a while, and I take a walk to give her some space. When we finally meet up again, Abby's eyes are filled with tears. "At least she's with her Abigail now. She can explain everything she needs to and finally be at peace."

When we pull up to the coffee shop, it's more crowded than I have ever seen it. "What is going on here today? Our table better be open! I've never seen it like this."

"I don't think that will be a problem," Abby grins. "I *might* have called Jessie earlier to ask her to keep our table open. She *might* have gotten excited and told a few friends we are back in town."

"Uh-huh." I give her a side-eyed glance, not buying the accidental nature of her slip of information.

We get out of the car, and one look inside the door tells me we might not even make it to our table in the back corner. There is barely enough room to stand. We pass an overflow of people sipping their coffee in the parking lot. I glare over at Abby. "You know I hate all the nonsense that comes with big crowds, right?"

Abby gasps, feigning offense. "I did all this for you!" My continued side-eye makes her quickly amend her statement. "Okay, for us… okay, mostly for us but also a little for me. I haven't seen my people in months! What better way to get back into society than to have all our neighbors, friends, coworkers—or former coworkers in my case—get together at our favorite place. Come on! It's going to be fun!" She links her arm through mine and practically skips into the building.

Our table is, in fact, reserved, and our usual coffee order is already waiting for us on the table. We have to push our way through the crowd, but we do make it over. Jessie spots us as soon as we sit down.

She greets us with hugs that would rival any grandmother's and kisses us both on the head. "Girls, how are you doing?"

Abby starts explaining everything, giving Jessie as few of the gruesome details as possible. She doesn't tell her about Victoria. I chime in here and there, but it's mostly Abby's story to tell.

I only interject with the juicy details Abby leaves out, like, "Did you see her new tattoo?"

"Yes, of course! The Phoenix. How fitting!" Jessie replies with a quick smile at Abby.

When Abby finishes telling the story, Jessie points at me and tells her, "Well, let me tell you, you are lucky to have this one. She just would not quit on you. When everyone was saying you were a runaway, or that you didn't exist," Jessie balks at the idea— "whatever that was all about, this girl had your back from the very first second something seemed amiss."

"Thanks, Jessie." Abby smiles to herself, and then at me. "No one could've hand-picked me a better sister." We both giggle, sharing an inside joke Jessie doesn't fully understand.

I look at Abby, confusion suddenly coloring my features. "What's so fitting about a phoenix?" The way Jessie looked at Abby when she said it piqued my interest.

"It's a symbol for rebirth and resurrection," she shrugs as if that explains everything. "Like starting a new chapter, reinventing yourself. I think parts of the old Abby are gone. Finding out who I was felt like a new birth. And I just wanted to make some physical changes in case Scott or anyone else was looking for me. Hence the haircut."

Abby stops suddenly and stretches her body to look over my head, fixated on something. The previous conversation is over, I guess. "Hmm, is there a reason Aiden is carrying your purse?"

"What?" I almost yell. How did he even know where I would be?

Reading my thoughts, Abby adds, "Oh, I told him where you'd be. Just not sure why he's holding your purse." She scrunches her eyebrows together.

"You did *what?*"

"It looked like he had something very important to ask you earlier. Although, you may just want to ask him. I'm not sure he'll be able to get the words out." Abby could not have looked prouder of herself if I caught her physically patting herself on the back.

"My purse was stolen. They must've found it at the house," I grumble as I stand up and push my way through the crowd again.

"Aiden, hi! Again." I greet him as I approach.

"Your sister told me you'd be here," he says, his cheeks blushing again.

"Yes, remind me to thank her for that later."

"I have your purse. It was recovered at the house. I meant to bring it with me this morning, but I forgot."

He's nervous again, a side of him I haven't seen all week. Was Abby right?

"There's something extra in it. A small birthday gift," he explains. I blink at him, confused, and he quickly adds, "It was your birthday this week. And a pretty crappy one at that."

I lose all ability to speak then.

He got me a birthday gift.

As I begin unwrapping the small box I find inside, Aiden begins stumbling over his words again. "Look, I'm- I'm just going to ask- I'm just- sorry I don't know why I'm-"

I raise a hand to stop him. "Aiden, do you want to join Abby and me for coffee?"

Relief floods his expression, as though a thousand-pound weight has been lifted off his shoulders. "I would love to." He smiles, reminiscent of the night we first met. While there was skepticism then, now there's only excitement and nerves, but the smile is the same.

"You don't do this very often, do you?" I laugh.

"Ask women out after working a case for them, outside my jurisdiction and against my boss's wishes? Not typically, no. I was afraid you might slap me if I asked any sooner. Bad timing and all that. I guess in my mind that's still a possibility now. This is not very professional of me," he admits sheepishly.

I finish unwrapping the gift box and pull out a beautiful silver necklace with a small coffee cup charm. My heart swells.

"I know it's not much, but I had short noti…"

I cut him off by leaning in and kissing him right there in the middle of the bustling little café. When I pull back, I smile and say, "I've been wanting to do that practically the whole week. And this," I hold up the necklace, "is perfect. Thank you so much!"

Handing him the necklace, I lift my hair so he can help me put it on.

"So, did I need the gift, or would I have gotten the kiss anyway?"

"Oh, no. The gift absolutely sealed the deal. You would've been so screwed if you forgot my birthday." Turning back to him, I raise an eyebrow, trying my best to look stern, but I know he can see through it.

His deep laugh fills the crowded shop as we make our way back to the table, now hand in hand. I sit down and notice Abby has already pulled up two more chairs. Kara occupies one, and she gestures for Aiden to take the other. It seems Jessie has gone back to work.

"I knew you'd do it!" Kara exclaims.

Both Aiden and I say "Thanks," simultaneously, and then blush in unison.

Kara groans dramatically, lamenting, "God, you guys are perfect. Why does this never happen to me?"

I playfully throw a muffin at Kara, but she quickly reminds me of her concussion and argues that she should get a free pass on anything dumb she says.

"Alright, the next time Abby gets kidnapped, you get dibs on the hot cop," I promise.

"Woah, woah. Why can't Rachel get kidnapped?" Abby interjects.

"Nope," Kara protests, shaking her head. "Then the hot cop would go for you, Abby. Don't even argue because you know I'm right. It's just science."

Abby gestures in agreement, and Kara retaliates with another muffin toss in her direction.

As we all find ways to keep each other laughing, Jessie returns to refill coffee and join the conversation. Aiden holds my hand my hand, and I squeeze lightly, feeling reassured. He seamlessly jumps right into our banter, joking and laughing with what's left of my small but perfect family.

All the people who mean the most to me in the world are gathered around this little coffee shop table.

There is still so much ahead of us. Decisions for Abby to make, a house to clean out and sell, and people that we now have to figure out if we can trust or not. Complex emotions linger for both Abby and me to sort through. But in this moment, in our favorite spot, everything feels like it might just work out. As long as we have each other, we can face whatever comes next, together.

EPILOGUE – ONE WEEK LATER

ABIGAIL

I finish vacuuming the last bedroom in the house while Rachel loads up the car with the last of the "Donation" boxes. There is a women's shelter not too far out of the way of our apartment.

Rachel and I decided it was best for me to move in with her temporarily while I figure out my next move. It saves us both money and we enjoy having each other so close again. Of course, I made her pay for the broken window before I could move out of my apartment. I wasn't thrilled about that when I found out she wasn't actually joking, but my landlord understood the situation after some explaining. After reminding me that she never would've found the letter if she hadn't broken in, I eased up on her a bit more.

"Rach, I'm ready to go!" My shout echoes through the empty home.

"Okay, just have to get all of the cleaning supplies in the car and then that should be everything!"

I meet Rachel by the front door to help her load the supplies. "Do we know what happened to Glenn?" I ask, curious about his absence. We have been back here a few times this week and haven't seen any movement. For someone who rarely leaves the general vicinity of his house, his car hasn't been in his driveway at all.

"No, actually, I'm not sure."

"His garden in the front is a bit overgrown with weeds popping up. I can't imagine he would let that happen if he were here." I try to picture a time when I saw even one weed starting to form in his garden and come up short.

"No. No one's seen him. I don't know if he was picked up at the house or if he got away. Honestly, though, good riddance. I'll never be able to look at him the same again, anyway. It's better that I don't have to look at him at all."

"Hmm." I tread carefully before continuing. "I actually believe him a bit, though. I don't think he ever would've agreed in the beginning if he knew where it was going to end up. I just can't imagine a man who took that much care of us, who was best friends with Mom, could ever intentionally hurt us."

"Maybe, but he had to know what Scott was capable of if he was involved with him at all," Rachel argues.

"Maybe," I concede, unwilling to completely condemn Glenn. The memories of genuine friendship, guidance, and laughter we shared with him couldn't have been all fake.

Changing the subject, Rachel asks, "Hey, have you given any more thought to what you're going to do about your real family?"

"You *are* my real family." I retort sharply, a look passing between us that signals she should know better.

"You know what I mean, Abigail."

"I don't know," I shrug. "Scott confessed to everything, so my 'real parents' know that he kidnapped their daughter. My identity is still a secret, though. Some people from the Miami-Dade area reached out to me with their information but left the decision completely up to me. I guess because I'm an adult now, I can choose. I don't know. Or maybe because they don't technically have to claim that they found Victoria if everyone thinks I'm Abigail. I don't think they were told his reasoning for kidnapping Victoria or that Abigail was killed. It's not like they found a body or anything. I don't know how it all works, but I'm thankful for the time."

I realize I'm rambling, making excuses now. The uncertainty about my identity and my future weighs heavily on me, despite my sister's reassuring presence.

I pause, hesitating while I figure out how to word what I want to say next. I don't want to come off as irrational, but I continue anyway. "Part of me feels like I owe them something, to let them know that I'm okay, to show them I did fine for myself after all these years. But the other part of me is terrified that everything will change if I take that step. I don't want any more change than what I already have right now. I did try to find them when I was on my own for those few months. I didn't have many resources and couldn't find them. Even if I had found them, I don't know if I would've opened up that floodgate. I just didn't have much else to focus on at the time."

"Of course, this is your decision, and I understand your reservations," Rachel reassures me. "Nothing will ever change between us. We have each other, always. Whatever you decide and however it works out, I'll be here to help you through it."

I pull my sister into a hug and say, "Alright, let's get out of here."

We bid farewell to the house where we grew up, filled with our favorite memories, where we struggled, laughed, cried, and grew up together.

Back at Rachel's apartment after yet another coffee stop, she changes while I turn on the TV. The lack of privacy and always having to change in the bathroom might get a little old, but right now, I am ecstatic to be in the same space as my sister again, especially after months apart.

"I'm starving!" I call out. "Pizza and movies tonight?"

"I'll take ham!" Rachel shouts back.

"That's disgusting!" I crinkle my nose, though she can't see me.

I walk over to the kitchen table where my phone is sitting and start dialing the number for the pizza place down the street. I'm pretty sure they deliver… Before anyone picks up, I catch a glimpse of a major news alert on the TV. It seems the TV automatically turns on a local news station, and I haven't changed the channel yet.

I walk closer to the TV to see what's going on and lose my grip on the phone. It falls to the floor, and the corner of the screen shatters. But I don't care. I can't muster the energy to care.

When I can find my voice, I scream, "RACHEL!"

Rachel rushes out of the bathroom, still half-dressed. "What? What's wrong? Are you okay?" She's panicking.

All I can do is point at the TV as the woman on the screen starts speaking.

"We bring to you tonight a special news alert. The body of a young child was discovered when maintenance workers came in to prepare this Westchester home for sale. The house sat unoccupied for nearly twenty years before the owner kidnapped and held two young ladies hostage there earlier this week. The body is believed to be none other than 1-year-old Victoria Wright, who went missing back in April of 2003.

"I have with me here a woman who lives in this neighborhood, just a few houses down, with her oldest daughter and grandchildren…"

I drown out the rest. I'm still watching the woman speak, but her words no longer register. I look to Rachel for guidance, but she's already dialing Aiden's number on her phone.

I run to the kitchen sink and throw up, unable to make it to the bathroom in time.

When Aiden arrives a little while later, he tells us he doesn't have much more information than we do. It appears that when

Evelyn accidentally killed Abigail, Scott buried the body in the backyard near the garden. There hasn't been any discussion about bringing people in to clean up the place, so it's possible Scott orchestrated this, wanting the information to come out.

"This is going to change everything," I think I say the words out loud, but they can't be more than a whisper. The weight of this news is slowly settling on my shoulders.

"Abby, we will get this sorted out. Neither of you will be implicated in any of this. I will do what I can to keep your identity yours for as long as you need," Aiden reassures us, his voice firm and determined, sounding more confident than he should.

The three of us sit around for the rest of the night, hoping against hope that this is all just a bad dream.

Milton Keynes UK
Ingram Content Group UK Ltd.
UKHW030658151124
451186UK00005B/61